Mrs. H. Grattan Guinness

Congo Recollections

Edited from notes and conversations of missionaries

Mrs. H. Grattan Guinness

Congo Recollections
Edited from notes and conversations of missionaries

ISBN/EAN: 9783337244903

Printed in Europe, USA, Canada, Australia, Japan

Cover: Foto ©Andreas Hilbeck / pixelio.de

More available books at **www.hansebooks.com**

CONGO RECOLLECTIONS.

*EDITED
FROM NOTES AND CONVERSATIONS
OF MISSIONARIES.*

BY

MRS. H. GRATTAN GUINNESS,

*Hon. Sec. of the East London Institute for Home and Foreign Missions,
Harley House, Bow, E.*

London:
HODDER AND STOUGHTON.
27, PATERNOSTER ROW.
MDCCCXC.

BUTLER & TANNER,
THE SELWOOD PRINTING WORKS,
FROME, AND LONDON.

PREFACE.

THE following recollections of some of our dear Congo missionaries may serve to bring men and incidents in this part of Central Africa before the minds of those who are interested in the Dark Continent.

Mr. Harvey went out ten years ago, and Mr. McKittrick about six years ago. Both were connected with the *Livingstone Inland Mission*, which was the first to take the gospel into this region. Its earliest members landed at Banana in January, 1878, just after Stanley's journey through the Dark Continent had made known to the world the vast entrance to Central Africa from the west. This Mission —which in 1884 was transferred to the *American Baptist Missionary Union*, in Boston—has borne already most encouraging fruit. Several native Churches, with hundreds of converts—numbers of whom are themselves preachers of the gospel—are now connected with it.

Mr. J. McKittrick has become leader in a new English extension of the Mission, on to the southern tributaries of this mightiest river of Africa. It is called the *Congo-Balolo Mission*, and its sphere of labour is the country of the Balolo-speaking people, who occupy the great horse-shoe bend of the Congo, and are supposed to number about ten million. The first party of missionaries for this new field started in April, 1889. Two stations are already occupied on the Lulonga and Maringa rivers, and eleven missionaries connected with this effort are now in Africa, and a third will be opened this spring. A steamer called the *Pioneer* has been sent out for the use of the Mission. It is intended to found stations also on the Juapa, the Ikelemba, and the Bosira.

It is difficult for civilized Europeans to realize what life in Central Africa is like, and it is still harder for Christian people to conceive heathen existence. We ought however to try and understand it, in order that we may sympathise, pity, and help. May these sketches enable some readers to do so!

Further information can be obtained from our larger work on the same subject, "The New World of Central Africa."

Who would not like to help to carry the light from heaven into the darkness of Africa?

HARLEY HOUSE, BOW,
LONDON, E.

CONTENTS.

MEN AND MANNERS ON THE CONGO. KING KANGAMPAKA AND THE KROO-BOYS. THE NATIVE MIND AND THE GOSPEL. THE CONGO TELEPHONE. A WALK IN BALOLOLAND. A CHAT WITH MR. RICHARDS, OF BANZA MANTEKA.

CHAPTER I.

KING KANGAMPAKA AND THE KROO-BOYS.

A CONGO KING.

THE following chapter contains recollections by Mr. Charles Harvey, of Lukunga, who first went out in 1880, and is still on the Congo. He was married to a missionary, Miss Harris, and had the sorrow of losing his wife.

THE name of the old chief of Palabala was Kangampaka or Nkangampaka. He was a very shrewd man, apparently about sixty years old, but, like most Africans, he had no idea of his own age; for once, when asked how old he was, he said that he believed he was "about twenty."

He was very polite to all white men; in fact, his politeness was pushed so far as to be an annoyance to any one unacquainted with the ways of African chiefs. When visited by a white man, he would send a slave for a chair for the guest, while he would sit on an empty gin box. He would then bring out some palm wine, or *malavu mamputu* (trade gin) if his visitor would take it, inquiring in the meantime, with much apparent concern, respecting his health, etc., etc.; and as it was contrary to etiquette to ask him to state the purpose of his visit, the guest could choose his own time for this, and could speak as long as he chose without fear of interruption, unless anything was mentioned that required explanation.

The old man, however, broke down signally on one occasion, and completely forgot his dignity.

In company with Mr. Picton, I was paying him a visit, after a long absence. An elderly man, a stranger to me, was present in the courtyard, seated near to the chief. Kangampaka was making a speech to this man, full of nauseating compliments respecting myself, when suddenly the old stranger fell forward on his face in an epileptic fit. The king became at once very excited, and, invoking the aid of his *nkissi*, or fetish, he cried out loudly again and again, "Catch his spirit! catch his spirit!" The courtyard in a few minutes was filled with men all armed with guns, whilst on the outside of the fence were women and children with terrified faces trying to peep over and ascertain the cause of the disturbance. Kangampaka at once told the men who ran in that the wicked old stranger who was lying struggling on the ground had endeavoured to work evil upon him, but that his own *nkissi* was too powerful for him, and had found him out. I could easily see, by the way he was looking at the man, his face being full of horror and hatred, that he meant mischief to the stranger; I therefore rose, and, addressing the king, told him that the man was only ill, and was not necessarily a bad man. The old chief here interrupted me, saying, very rudely, that it was none of my business, but that this was a matter that must be settled Fiote fashion. I knew, of course, that this would mean death to the poor old stranger, so I insisted upon being heard, telling the king that in our country we knew all about that sickness, for we had plenty of people who were taken ill in the same way, and some of them were very good people. I further told him that God would be angry if he took away the man's life because he was sick, and not only would he have to answer to God in the other world, but to man in this world, if he did not let the poor fellow alone. I could see that he felt himself in a dilemma, but he thought for a minute or two, and at length said,—

"You say you know all about this sickness in your country; well then, if so, give him medicine to cure him, and then we shall know that it is a sickness."

I at once accepted the challenge, believing that the fit could not last very long, and that a little brandy would do him no harm. Leaving Picton to watch events, I started off to the mission house to procure it, and in the meantime the man came to, and was allowed to depart unharmed.

Kangampaka was of a very revengeful disposition, especially towards those he considered to be the enemies of his town.

On one occasion he came to me and asked for some of that stuff like Bula Matari (Stanley) used in blowing up some rocks near Vivi—dynamite, of course. Being curious to know why he wanted it, I asked him, and he said: "Those Noki people are bad people. Give me some of that stuff like Bula Matari has, and I will put some under their hill, and blow them all into the air."

He laughed very incredulously when I told him that I had none, and added that if I *had*, I should not dare to give it to him for such a dreadful purpose, as God had told us to love our enemies—not to blow them in the air! He looked hard at me, as much as to say, "Do you white men really believe in loving enemies?" I fancy that he had a difficulty in reconciling such a creed with the big cannon of which he had heard!

The old man had a very great veneration for a book or anything written. I was obliged to take advantage of this one day.

It happened that we had cut down some trees in a sacred wood near the station, which displeased the chiefs very much. My first intimation of this was by a messenger, who said, "The chief is angry, and is coming to see you." Soon afterwards the old man and two other chiefs arrived. He tried very carefully to explain that *he* was my friend, and not at all displeased with me, but that a number of other chiefs were very angry, not only with me, but also with him, for not being angry with me in the matter of the desecration of the sacred wood.

HENRY CRAVEN, OF LIVERPOOL,
THE FIRST MISSIONARY TO THE CONGO.
SAILED IN JAN., 1878; DIED AT KABINDA, OCT. 14TH, 1884.

I replied that I was so glad he had not sided with the other chiefs, for now the matter would be very simple, for if he would only tell me their names, I would see about it. So getting a large sheet of paper and pen and ink, I asked him to tell me the name of the first, that I might *write it down*. This evidently caused much consternation, for there was a good deal of whispering among them. They had not calculated upon this. Who could foresee what might come about if names were put in a letter? After a few minutes, the king said, "Don't write anything down, white man. The matter is settled!" And I never heard any more of it!

Kangampaka was very fond of Craven, and would do anything for him, *except give his heart to God*, and this of course was what Craven desired most of all. At times there seemed to be a probability that he would yield, for undoubtedly more than once he was under serious concern for his soul; but there was one thing that hindered, and that was *the white man's drink!*

Long before he knew the missionary the old man had acquired a craving for the fiery spirit sold by the lower river traders, and no inducement could persuade him to give it up. On this point he was all along openly at variance with the missionaries, and he considered that Craven's only fault was refusing to supply him with gin. Craven made very earnest and persistent efforts to reclaim him from the power of this curse, and often sent coffee to the king's house (when he had promised to try and give up the drink),

AN AFRICAN GRAVE, WITH BROKEN CROCKERY.

hoping that it would be substituted for the wretched gin; but, alas! the demon prevailed, for up to the day of his death, twelve months ago, he was, body and soul, the slave of drink.

In accordance with Congo custom, his body was kept for a long time in the house in which he had died, until sufficient cloth had been given by his relatives and friends to wind around the corpse, and bury with him. After months had elapsed, and an enormous quantity been contributed, the funeral took place; but by this time the body with its multitudinous wrappings resembled a large hogshead, painted over with a number of strange devices. He was buried in a great pit which was dug close to the spot where he had so long conducted both his court and his revels.

Poor, guilty, and yet victimized Kangampaka! He could never bear to *hear* of the resurrection of the dead, yet *rise again he must!* But who in that great day would not rather be the drunken heathen chief than the so-called Christian trader, with blood-guiltiness for the ruin of that old man, among thousands of others, upon his soul? Beyond all doubt trade-gin was the stumbling-block that kept him from Christ. The fascination of the drunkard's delirious paradise was too great for the morally weak and helpless heathen to resist. Woe to those who lured him,—and are daily luring thousands like him—to degradation, ruin, and death, for the sake of selfish gain!

AN N'GANGA, OR MEDICINE-MAN.

Houses at Palabala.

The first house put up at Palabala was built of native material almost entirely, the only exception being the doors and windows, which were made out of Morton's provision boxes!

The roof was thatched with dried grass, but the thatching was not well done, and there was considerable leakage in various places during the tornadoes which occurred at least every other day in the wet season.

When the first sound of a storm came, waterproofs ground sheets, and mackintoshes would be brought out to cover everything that could spoil or be damaged by wet, such as beds, blankets, and books. Where the leakage was very bad, pails would be placed underneath, to prevent large pools forming on the floors of the various rooms. But what was to be dreaded more than tornadoes was a fog or Scotch mist, such as frequently enveloped the Palabala hill, which was 1,700 feet high. The walls of the house being made only of papyrus-mats, were more useful for ventilation than for protection from the weather. It was no unusual thing to go to bed, the stars shining brightly outside, and to wake very early in the morning, feeling shivery and uncomfortable. If the matches were not too damp, a light would be struck, and then the cause of the trouble would be only too apparent, for the room would be seen to be full of a thick fog which would chill one to the bone. During the night the clouds had gathered, and one black,

COMFORTLESS CONDITIONS. 19

dense rain-cloud had struck the hill and penetrated everywhere. In the morning, boots, socks, trousers Bible, everything, would be clammy and damp.

What wonder therefore that we all, without exception, had many fevers, or that some of our number died! That so many escaped, although usually with broken health, was the surprising thing. Such risks as we ran by living in so poor and unsuitable a house should, if possible, be avoided, even at the beginning of a local work, and, with sufficient resources, experience, and due foresight, they can and ought to be.

Some little time before the present iron house was put up, matters began to assume a very bad appearance as regards the safety of the old house and of the out-houses.

One day, while a tornado was raging, we heard

above the storm a loud noise succeeded by screams of terror from the children.

"The cook-house must be blown down," said Craven.

I ran to the nearest door, but I was an invalid and not strong at that time, and as it faced the storm and opened outwards, the storm completely mastered me. Try all in my power, I could not open that door! In the meantime Craven had got through a side door, and was overjoyed to find that although the cook-house had indeed fallen, it had fallen over and round the poor frightened children, and had not hurt a single one of them. Our evening worship that day became a service of praise!

The next tornado after this nearly brought the dwelling-house down about our own ears. It was a very wild storm. The lightning was terrible, flash succeeding flash with hardly any intermission. The wind roared and shrieked among the trees of the plantation close by, while the thunder boomed and crashed incessantly. The wall on the storm side of the station began to sway. It seemed as if any moment might see us buried beneath the ruins of the house. Craven called to me, shouting at the top of his voice because of the storm, "We had better get into the store: it's safer there! Where is Johnson?" I found Johnson in his room watching with dismay the swaying wall I laid hold of him, and said, "Come along"; but he protested, "Wait, wait; I believe the house will come down." As this seemed to me to be an urgent reason why we should *not* wait, I pulled him forcibly out ; but just then one of the sudden lulls peculiar to tropical tornadoes came, and we were saved for that time.

Soon after this the old house was propped and shored up, which proved sufficient to keep it from being blown down until it was superseded by a good corrugated iron structure, built on a site a little distance away. In this there is no need to fear rain, fog, or storm, although it is built in a much more exposed position than was the old house.

THE KROO-BOY.

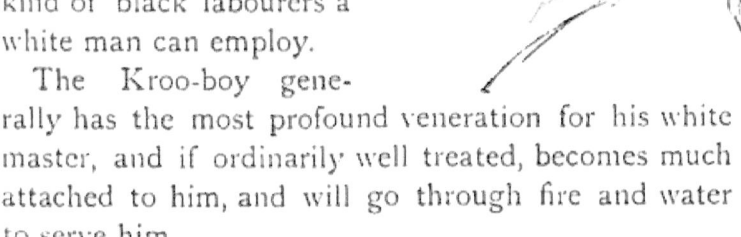

In the early stages of the mission's history the natives could not be depended upon for labour of any kind, so it became necessary to hire Kroo-boys (or Kroo-men, for they are usually full-grown men) from the Guinea Coast, and these have proved themselves to be the best kind of black labourers a white man can employ.

The Kroo-boy generally has the most profound veneration for his white master, and if ordinarily well treated, becomes much attached to him, and will go through fire and water to serve him.

He will work from sunrise to sunset at the hardest

CARRIERS CROSSING A RIVER.

kind of labour, such as carrying stones to make the foundation for a house, or puddling clay to make walls. He will work quite cheerfully, and will be thoroughly satisfied with about a pound of rice, or a few heads of maize, and some plantains per day, with the addition of some fish or meat once or twice a week. If required (and of course he is not by missionaries), he is quite willing to shoulder a gun and fight his master's enemies with much bravery if his master will only lead him ; or he will without a murmur (or, at the most, with a murmur) throw down his spade or pick, and within a quarter of an hour start on a journey of a hundred miles, carrying a load of sixty pounds weight, with the addition of his own rations for the journey. All this he will do for about 6*d.* or 9*d.* per day and his food.

The Kroo-boy usually discards his own name, and adopts one given to him by the purser of the steamer or others, probably on account of the unpronounceability of the Kroo-names by the unfacile English tongue. The distribution of these names is often very facetious, and not unseldom positively ludicrous. Sometimes when a Kroo-boy is asked his name, he will give " Jim Crow," " Snowball," " Red Herring," or even " Frying Pan " or " Pea Soup." It sounds very comical when a messenger comes and tells you that " Jim Crow " has been pitching into " Pea Soup," or that " Frying Pan " won't give up the cooking pot, or has insulted poor "Tea Kettle" by calling him a black bushman.

Although he is intelligent, the Kroo-boy is by no means highly civilized, and appliances puzzle him. At a certain station a quantity of earth had to be carried from a pit to make a foundation for a house, and a wheelbarrow was introduced to save time and labour. The Kroo-boy loaded the barrow very carefully, and then stood still, scratched his head, and

KROO "BOYS" IN THE WATER.

looked completely mystified. What was to be done next? In a minute or two he had solved the problem, and walked away with the loaded wheelbarrow *on the top of his head!*

The Kroo-boy is very ready to listen to Christian teaching, but his language is the great hindrance to a communication of the gospel message to him, while his own knowledge of the English tongue is extremely imperfect. The medium generally employed is a kind of "pidgin English," which hardly answers the purpose of conversing upon the ordinary affairs of life; consequently when the sublime truths of the gospel are the subject, its poverty and imperfectness is but too apparent; nevertheless some eternal impressions have doubtless been made upon the hearts of these poor simple-minded heathen servants. The missionary, indeed, has a choice between speaking good English to one of their number, who understands better than his neighbours, and can translate into Kroo—and speaking in broken English, such as the Kroo-boys themselves use. The latter is usually preferred, as the interpreter cannot be followed, and cannot be detected when he has misapprehended and misrepresented truth; but the difficulties are very great either way.

The following is a specimen of Kroo-boy English, and is, as will be seen, a paraphrase of the " Prodigal Son."

"One man live for dem other country, he catch two boy.

"Dem young boy he say to him father, 'I no fit to stop here. I fit to go far 'way; give me cloth.'

"Him father he feel sick for heart; he no want 'm go, but dem boy he say, 'I go.'

"Dem boy, he go for road, he sleep plenty night for path, den he see one town, he say, 'I fit to stop here.'

"Dem men for dat town sabby (know) plenty cheat, dem boy he buy palm wine, he buy gin, he buy pig he give dem men. Every night, plenty, plenty dance.

"One day he look in box, no see cloth; cloth finish.

"Dem men for town dey say, 'We no catch cloth for you. Go 'way.'

"Dem boy he no catch kwanga, no catch plantain; he live for die! (*i.e.* he is about to die).

"He see one man, he say, 'I fit to work for you, massa.' Dem man he say, 'All right. Pigs dere, live for field, go keep 'm.'

"Dem boy he go, he see pig's chop (pig's food), him 'tummack too much sick (faint with hunger), he chop 'm (ate some).

"Dem boy he say, 'All dem Kroo-boy (servants) for my father catch plenty chop. I no fit to stop here. 'Spose I stop here, den I live for die' (I shall die).

"He sleep plenty nights for road, den he see dem house for him father. Him father he look, he look, he say, 'My boy he live for come' (just coming).

"He run plenty ; he look dat boy, he kiss 'm.

"Dem boy he say to 'm father, 'I be bad too much ; I no be chile for you any more. I fit to be Kroo-boy (servant) for you.'

"Him father he say to dem boy, 'You come 'long.'

"Dem father he tell dem Kroo-boy, 'You go catch calf. Make plenty chop (food). You sabby (know) dis boy come back? All same 'spose he come back from grave. We fit to dance plenty to-night.'"

CENTRAL AFRICAN POTTERY.

CHAPTER II.

THE CONGO TELEPHONE.

TELEPHONIC communication is by no means one of the new things under the sun, especially under the tropical Congo sun; for the various tribes dwelling on the banks of the Congo, both on the upper and lower river, have for ages had a very complete system of telegraphing by sound, or telephoning as it is called. They are perfectly able to communicate in this way any word or sentence; anything, in fact, which they are able to speak themselves, they can transmit to towns a long distance off, but which are within hearing distance.

This communication is effected by means of a kind of drum, which is made of very hard wood, hollow throughout, and varying in thickness so that when struck from the inside, as many as four different tones or sounds can be produced.

The operator holds in each hand a drum-stick; and by varying the intervals between the beats upon the different toned sides of the drum, an almost infinite variety of signals can be conveyed to the ear. Usually the natives take this drum down to the water's edge, as they know by practical experience that sound travels much farther over water surface than over land. The town is first "called," and when reply is made the message to be conveyed is beaten out syllable by syllable. But its uses are by no means confined to communication with neighbouring towns, but far more frequently it is employed for local purposes; for instance, the drum will suddenly sound out the name of some individual who belongs to the same town and who is perhaps in the forest hard by, or at the mission station; and he is told that his chief wants to speak to him, or his wife may intimate that dinner is *quite* ready, or a trusting friend will publicly advise him that he will be very glad of repayment of the fifty brass rods borrowed in the more or less remote past, and so on.

In the Cataract Region, in towns away from the river, the natives communicate with other towns chiefly at night, when everything is so still and quiet that the cry of the jackal or the hooting of the owl can be heard many miles away.

At Palabala they carry the drum to the side of the hill when they wish to send a message to Nokki, a town on a neighbouring hill, but which is six to seven miles off as the crow flies. After some amount of beating in a peculiar irregular way, they pause; and the sound of an answering drum at Nokki can be distinctly, though faintly heard. Then some words or part of message is telephoned, and the answering

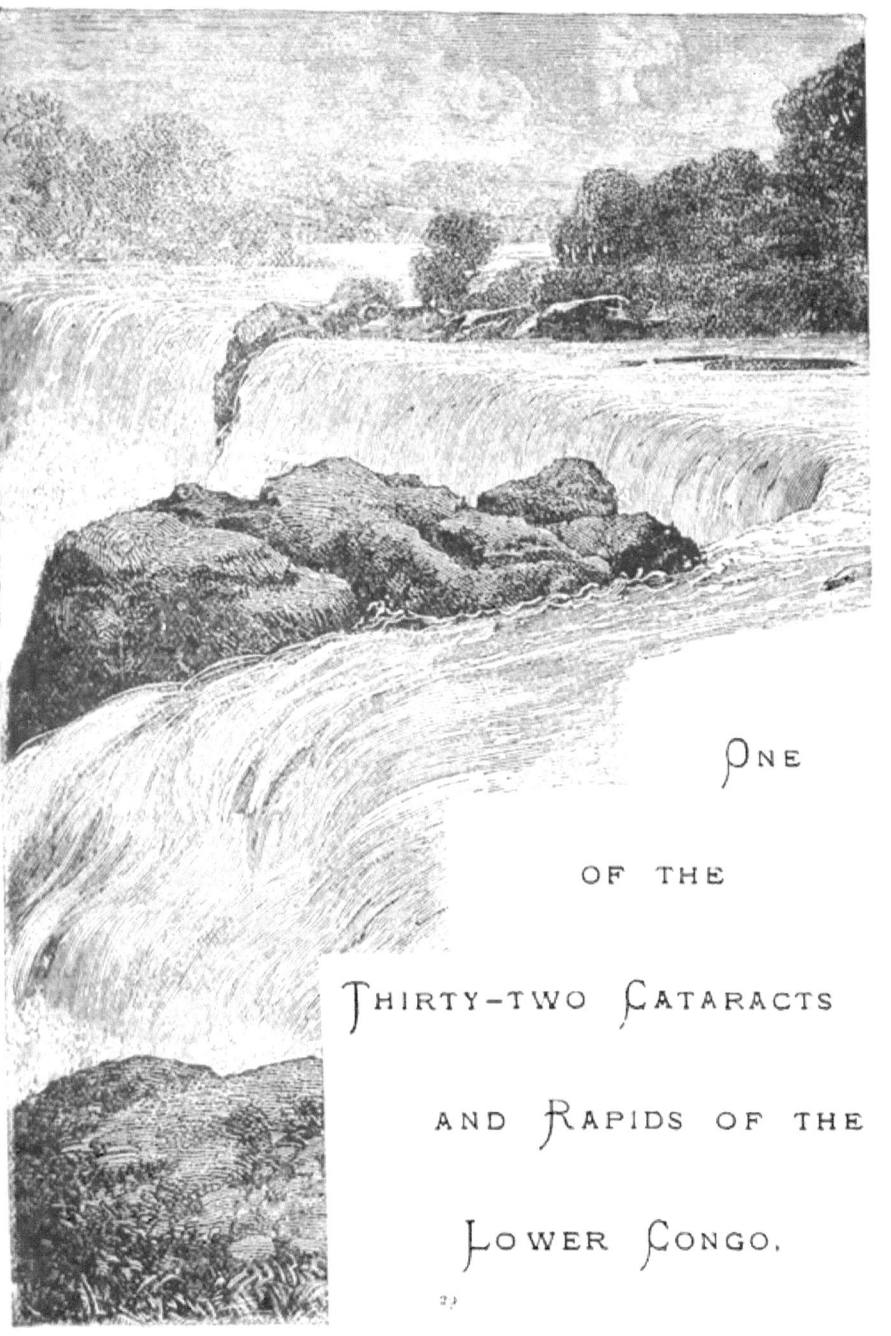

One of the Thirty-two Cataracts and Rapids of the Lower Congo.

signal "all right" is given after each pause. Then the Palabala drum will stop, and the Nokki drum beat out some reply, to which the responses will be given in due order.

These drums are especially valuable in time of dispute or war; for an international question can be argued under the very best possible conditions, when every one is calm, and the wit and wisdom of each town fully available to assist negotiations. In case of an attack being intended upon a neighbouring town, due notice would be given as a matter of course by means of the drum, and the day and the time of the day (or position of the sun) duly notified when the attack might be expected!

The missionaries at the Equator Station had once practical evidence of the usefulness of the telephone drum, and of the fulness and accuracy of the news conveyed by it.

Before starting upon an expedition to towns not previously visited, Mr. McKittrick had engaged the services of a drummer. This man would take his station in the fore part of the canoe, and some time before they got to a town he would tell the people all about the missionary, how peaceable his errand was, and the good things he had to tell them. Consequently, instead of an armed, suspicious crowd to meet them at the landing-place, the chiefs and the people would be waiting to accord them a hearty welcome. In this way quite a number of towns were visited without danger to the missionary or the people who accompanied him. One day, while returning to Equator-

THE LANGUAGE.

ville, but several miles away, the drummer conveyed to the natives at the station tidings of the doings of the expedition, the names of the towns visited, the substance of what the chiefs said, the shooting of a hippopotamus, and other incidents. All this the people told the missionary left in charge of the station before his colleague arrived, and it was found by comparison to agree in every particular with the facts.

Who can say to what other uses this valuable means of communication may yet be brought? May it not reasonably be hoped, that in time to come other messages than those of dispute and war will be conveyed, and the wonderful story of God's love to man, as shown by the gift of His only begotten Son, be the subject of many a message to many of the towns yet unevangelized, and especially to those which would not be disposed at first to permit a missionary to go among them. In this way not only an entire town, but often a number of towns, might at the same time listen to the " glad tidings of great joy," sounded forth on some Gospel Telephone Drum.

LINGUISTIC DIFFICULTIES.

The curse of the Tower of Babel is very specially realized by those whose duty and privilege it is to pioneer in a perfectly heathen and uncivilized country where the language has never been reduced to writing and where there are no interpreters of any kind.

If an Englishman travels abroad, in most parts of the world he is able to secure the services of an interpreter; he can carry a pocket dictionary, and by help of the literature of the country he can soon make himself understood. But in a land absolutely without dictionaries, grammars, or interpreters, the case is very different!

When we first landed on the Congo, communication with the natives was principally by pantomime, and the acquisition of the first little vocabulary was difficult and slow work.

THE CEREMONY OF MAKING PRESENTS, OR "DASH."

Let us suppose the missionary has just reached the country—fresh from Europe; his tent has been pitched not far from a Congo village, with a view to cultivating amicable relations with the people.

At first the natives seem very timid, and hardly dare to approach nearer than to be able to command a distant view of the camp. But the missionaries are both inside their tent, which emboldens some of the more venturesome of the people to hazard themselves a few yards nearer; but suddenly the canvas door of the tent is flung on one side, and out steps the man with the bogie-looking white skin (the native bogie is always white). Instantly there is a general panic, and young and old scamper away in terror, and hide themselves in the long grass. In a few minutes however they recover somewhat; and a few of the men, feeling a little ashamed of themselves, begin to cuff the small boys and demand very indignantly why they ran away from the white man.

But now the fowl-merchant makes his appearance, carrying on his head a long basket made of palm branches full of fowls. He ranks in public estimation as a very dreadnought, for he for years has made periodic excursions down the country right into the white man's lair for purposes of trade, and has always returned triumphantly, bearing rich spoils in the shape of handkerchiefs, beads, and bottles of the white man's palm wine (*malavu mamputu*), or gin. But even he keeps at a respectful distance, and places his fowls on the ground about a dozen yards from the tent. The missionary goes over to him, and at once the native addresses him in what is to him an unintelligible jargon. Which of that jumble of sounds is a word?

How impossible it seems to be, even to make a beginning with such a language!

The poor missionary shakes his head and looks helpless.

But one of the Kroo-boys, just fresh from the
C. R.

Guinea Coast, sees the situation, and although he does not understand a word of the native language, offers his services as interpreter.

"Any port in a storm," thinks the missionary. Besides, the responsibility of failure will be shifted, or at least divided, so he makes no objection.

"Snowball," the Kroo-boy (who by the bye is unusually black even for a Kroo-boy) says,—

"You fit to buy dem fowl, massa?"

"Yes, Snowball, I want to buy them."

"How much massa fit to give?"

"Oh, that depends. How much does he want?"

Snowball sidles over towards the native—who shrinks away a little, and looks as if he wishes he hadn't come—he then shouts in his ear: "Look'ee, you black bushman—dem fowl—how much?"

The native scratches his head and looks puzzled, then rattles away at a great rate in his own language as a kind of self-defence, which makes "Snowball" look perplexed in his turn. However he tries again, and taking four fowls out of the basket, he hands over a piece of cloth, which the native carefully examines, then proceeds to ascertain for how many fowls he is supposed to have been paid. He slowly counts twice over, *Imosi, iole, itatu, ia,* one, two, three, four. These are evidently some of the numerals, so the missionary repeats after him, as if counting himself, *Imosi, iole, itatu, ia,* to the delight of the native, who thinks he must know more of the language than he pretends. He consequently breaks forth in quite a tornado of eloquence; but his auditor by this time is carefully noting down "*imosi, iole, itatu, ia,*" and feels that whatever the four fowls may eventually cost him in cloth, they will be cheap with these adjectives thrown in.

But the fowl-merchant is evidently dissatisfied, for he takes up one of the fowls and puts it back in the basket, still keeping the cloth in his hand, repeating again and again, "*Nsusu zitatu, nsusu zitatu.*" The "*itatu*" is three, can "*nsusu*" be the word for fowl? It is put to the test, and after almost as much expenditure of breath as would be sufficient to capture an African butterfly, the word is caught, and duly transferred to the note-book always kept handy for that purpose.

KROO-BOY.

In the meantime the other natives have approached nearer and nearer, being unable to resist the temptation of seeing a bargain struck; for next to the pleasure of buying and selling personally, the Congo native enjoys looking on while others trade. The business is now at last completed, and the fowls sold at the rate of three for one piece of cloth ; and finally all parties go away satisfied, but none more so than "Snowball," who feels that he is getting on well with the native language, or, as he himself calls it, "dem bushman talk."

Still better opportunities of acquiring the language occurred during school teaching. The quick boys of the school soon discovered that the highway to favour with the teacher was to help him to get hold of words in their language ; and, indeed, the pleasure of being the teacher of the teacher—and that teacher a white man too—was so highly appreciated that it was freely indulged in by all.

But the teacher was compelled to be judicious in his employment of words and phrases thus acquired, otherwise it would neither minister to the edification nor to the discipline of the school. It was early discovered that the missionary would act wisely if he did his scolding in *English:* if not, he was in danger of breaking down in the middle of his expostulations in a ludicrous manner ; or he would perhaps express himself so funnily, that not only would the whole school be put in a roar, but even the culprit under reprimand has been known to fall from his seat and kick about on the floor in a fit of uncontrollable laughter, the unintended effect of solemn exhortations in broken Fiote. On the other hand, a little declamation in English usually produced an awed hush throughout the school, and the misdemeanant would look as if he never would dare to do the like again !

Common nouns were comparatively easy to get,

but verbs and words expressing abstract ideas very far from easy. Many of these last were only acquired after years of patient endeavour after them, or waiting for them to turn up. Even some quite ordinary words were not obtained until they had been sought for weeks. One missionary very soon got the word "to-morrow," but try all he would for a long time he was not able to get hold of "yesterday," until one day quite accidentally he heard it, and was able to secure it.

The tenses of the verbs were puzzling and easily mistaken. One of the missionaries, through systematically using a past tense which should only be used for things that have *just* happened, unwittingly gave the natives the idea that in some mystical sense Christ died for us *every day*.

The discovery of any but the principal and elementary rules of the grammar was a painfully slow process. The first attempt at a grammar was an elementary one by Rev. H. Grattan Guinness, which was published in 1882. This was soon after followed by a vocabulary of some three thousand words of the Palabala dialect by Rev. H. Craven, and two years ago Rev. W. Holman Bentley, of the English Baptist Mission, published a dictionary of the language as spoken at San Salvador, as well as some copious grammatical notes of very great value.

Some translation work has also been accomplished. Besides "Peep of Day" (an outline of Bible history for children), the four Gospels, the First Epistle of John, most of Genesis, and twenty chapters of Exodus, have been translated by various members of the mission; and quite recently the Acts of the Apostles has been rendered into Fiote by a native convert now studying in a college in America.

As the language has been reduced, it has been found to be exceedingly rich in inflexions; and owing to the native rule requiring all speakers at their "palavers" to employ only the highest class Fiote of which they are capable, the purity and integrity of the language has been remarkably preserved, at least in the interior.

There are many difficulties in translation peculiar to Africa, or to a tropical climate. For instance, the people have no idea of ice or snow, and consequently have no words for them. Their sheep, as a rule have no wool, but hair; and those which do have wool are *black*. In the interior they have not the least notion of the sea, and the only word that approaches the idea means the wide part of a river. They know, moreover, nothing of coin as currency, therefore Mr. Richards, in his version of Luke, has had to render the word "talents" in the parable as *pieces of cloth*. And in the verse where our Lord says: "Verily I say unto thee, Thou shalt in no wise come out until thou hast paid the uttermost farthing," "uttermost farthing" has been rendered "mother of the last blue beads," which is the exact equivalent in the Congo language!

It is somewhat discouraging to remember, that much as has been done towards giving the gospel to the African, it is almost nothing to what yet remains

AFRICAN DIALECTS.

to be accomplished. On the banks of the Congo and its tributaries alone, a considerable number of languages are spoken, as distinct as French and Italian, and requiring separate translation work. It is true that the mastery of one language will assist greatly in the reduction of the rest, as they all belong to the great Bantu family; but each requires separate study, and hence the need of many students. May God thrust forth more labourers into this great harvest field!

CHAPTER III.
THE NATIVE MIND AND THE GOSPEL.

THE natives have usually passed through three distinct stages in relation to the gospel before they have accepted it; *viz*. indifference, curiosity, and opposition. Each of these stages may have been of longer or shorter duration, and their order may not always have been exactly the same; but as far as our observation extends, the work at each of the stations has passed through them all before there has been anything like a general appreciation of the truth.

The first stage, indifference, extended over a long period of the early history of the Mission, and the cause is not difficult to discover.

Here were a few white men, for some time unable to communicate their message except in a poor broken Fiote ; much of their time taken up in house-building, travelling, transport of goods, etc. ; often very sick, and seldom quite well ; knowing little of the manners and customs, modes of thought and prejudices of the people ; foreign in speech, dress, ideas upon everything, and especially upon religion ; of course unbelievers in the traditions of their forefathers handed down from past generations, and wishful to supersede them by a religion that apparently forbad indulgence in almost all the chief pleasures and gratifications of life ! And when perhaps a little progress had been made, the white man's God had little attraction to the native mind ; for not only was He unable to keep them from being sick (the chief object of their own superstitious rites), but many of them had even been allowed to die. Where then was the advantage of such a religion as that, which was unable to help even its own propagators ?

At first, indeed, apparently, interest was displayed but it was only apparent, or rather, it was in the *white man*, and not in his message. There was the utmost desire to be on good terms with him, but the greatest indifference as to his God. They would meet and listen patiently while he discoursed in such broken, strange Fiote, that sometimes they thought that it must be the language of the white man's country to which they were listening! They would shut their eyes while he talked with his own eyes shut, into the air it seemed, but the white man said it was to Nzambi, the great God ; and they would say Amen at the end of it all, with much unction and fervour, but no further would they go. And, indeed, many of them believed that this was as far as they were expected to go, and would relate to the missionary, as quite commendable, that on the previous Saturday night they had attended a fetish dance, but that this did not make them neglect the meetings for the worship of Nzambi, evidently thinking it possible to serve God and Belial at the same time. (Not the only people who have made this mistake since the world began!)

But when at length they began to understand that God claimed nothing less than *themselves*, and would not be satisfied with anything they could do, they said quite candidly that that might be a good religion for the white man, but it was not suitable for the black man, who had different customs altogether, and *was* in himself different.

It was almost heart-breaking at times to go into the towns to preach, knowing that men, women, and children were hiding away, or to hear them make any excuse rather than listen to the word, or to see them standing listlessly by, as they patronisingly assented to the most heart-searching truths. Some would confess they were sinners, declare that they had repented, believed in Jesus, that they loved God with all their heart and soul, and were keeping all His commandments: and all the time we were morally certain their hearts were as dark as Satan and superstition could make them.

After this came the next stage—curiosity.

The unanimity of the testimony of the Mindele mia Nzambi (God's white men—a name they gave to the missionaries) was one of the causes of this. "You all speak the same thing," they said on more than one occasion. "It doesn't matter which missionary it is that comes here, all tell us the same story."

Then the lives of the missionaries, in contrast with those of many of the traders and others, impressed them. In Africa there must of necessity be very little private life. The white man has to be a "living epistle, known and read of all men," and it was especially *so* in the early history of the mission. *Then* almost every little word or act was watched, noted, and interpreted. Very little escaped their notice. Wherever we went, and whatever we did, there was sure to be a number of curious eyes and ears always open and ready to find in us anything inconsistent with our professed object in coming amongst them. And did we never fail then? Our pitiful Father in heaven, who knoweth our frame, knows how often. So often, indeed, that the remembrance should cause much humbleness of mind; and yet withal we have much cause to praise the grace that on the whole did keep us faithful and consistent under very trying conditions of bodily and spiritual life.

There was also another cause of native curiosity which should not be left out of the account. It was

NATIVE WOMAN HOEING.

"THE WHITE MAN IS a sign given by God Himself,—*rain sent in answer to prayer*, and it attracted much attention.

The rainy season had come, but no rain! The women had sown their seed, and the blade had appeared; but as one month and then nearly another passed over, and not a shower visited the earth and watered it, the green shoot began to turn yellow, and the young crops flagged and drooped. Another month or two of such drought, and famine would be the consequence. In their distress they tried the rain fetish.

One evening, as one of the missionaries was taking his usual walk, passing through the town, he heard the beating of a drum, and seeing one of the mission school lads, he asked what it meant, and was told that the people were to assemble that night and dance for rain.

The missionary said to the lad: "But *you* know that will not bring rain, don't you?"

"Oh, yes, teacher, it will."

"Nonsense! How can beating a drum and dancing make the rain to fall? If God wants it to rain, it will, but not otherwise."

"Ah, well, teacher, you will see. Just notice now if it does not rain before to-morrow morning."

That evening walk was saddened by the conversation held with the lad. How dark everything seemed! After years of toil and prayer, not only were the people as much wedded to their superstition as ever, but even hopeful scholars of the mission school were still in gross darkness and believing lies. Alas! this heathenism! What a dreadful, real power it seemed to be! When would the people be delivered from the bondage of its yoke? "O God!" groaned out the missionary, "forbid that Thy rain should fall in apparent response to their invocation of devils! Keep back Thy clouds until they seek the blessing from THEE."

That night and many others passed, and no rain came. Notwithstanding all the drumming and dancing, the clouds were obstinate, and would not obey the most powerful spells. More than two months of the rainy season had now gone by, and no drop of rain had fallen. Scarcity, disease, and death, such as the old men said had come upon the land in former days, seemed to be impending. But why was it? Who was the cause of the drought? who was it that was hindering the rain from coming? The conversation of the boy with the white man was reported. Yes, that was it! That was why their medicine-men could do nothing. *The white man was stopping the rain!*

The news soon spread, "The white man it is who is stopping the rain," and the rage of the people—especially the women—was very great. Had it been one of themselves, and not a white man, his life would not have been worth many hours' purchase. But a white man was different! To kill him would mean bringing unknown dangers upon the whole community. And, moreover, the king protected him! Let Kangampaka protest then against this bad conduct to the white man himself, and perhaps when he knows that he is found out he will let the rain come.

The king thereupon sent his headman to the suspected missionary, and told him that all the people,

A CONGO WOMAN.

especially the women, were very angry with him, believing him to be keeping back the rain from them. The missionary replied that it was not he, but the people themselves.

"How was that?"

"Just this way. God owns all the clouds, for He made them. Season by season He has sent the rain to you unasked, and you have had plenty to eat in all your towns. But who among you have ever once thanked *Him*? Instead of doing that, you have done that which He abominates in praising and thanking your rain fetish."

"What then shall we do, white man?"

Here was a most practical question! How ought it to be answered? There seemed to be but one way, and that to take up the challenge of the heathen chief in God's name.

"Tell Kangampaka," replied the missionary, "to appoint a day for all the people to come together, and wait upon God to give them rain; and if they come to Him with sincere hearts, and put away their fetishes, He will hear them."

The answer came back very soon. "The words of the white man are good. The king appoints to-morrow."

The morrow came, and the people flocked in large numbers to the little church, which was full to overflowing; chiefs and people from all the adjacent towns were there. After some exhortation prayer was offered, and the people dispersed.

All through the rest of that day the missionaries agonised in prayer to God, and towards evening the answer seemed to be at hand, for thick, black clouds rolled overhead, but, alas! dispersed again.

It was a sore trial of faith, but still they prayed on, and gave the Lord no rest. Through that night they watched and prayed, and before the dawn of the next day the clouds came overhead again, and this time did not disperse until a glorious, refreshing shower had fallen upon the thirsty land.

In the morning the king himself came to the station and asked, "What shall we do now?"

"Come together again to thank God for what He has sent, and ask Him for more," was the reply.

They came, but not nearly in such large numbers as at first. Alas poor human nature! However public prayer was offered once again, and within a few hours more rain fell. During the evening however the missionaries heard the noise of a drum in the town. What could it be? Upon inquiry they found it was *a dance in honour of the rain fetish!*

It was some weeks before another shower of rain descended upon that plateau, but they had received an unmistakable sign from the Lord, unmistakable to all but the wilfully blind; and now sufficient rain was sent to give them a second crop and prevent starvation.

NATIVES COMING FOR MEDICINE TO THE MISSIONARY'S TENT.

CHAPTER IV.

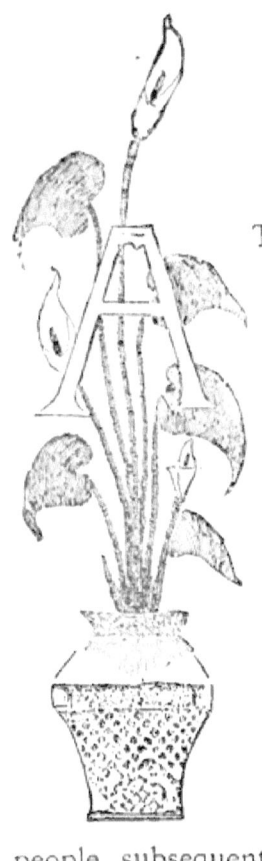

AT Banza Manteka a few weeks afterwards a like event occurred; but in that case the natives themselves asked to be allowed to meet and pray for rain, having doubtless heard what had taken place at Palabala. They met at the mission house, when Mr. Richards exhorted them to receive the truth of God. Nkoiyo, a converted scholar, and Lutete, the first Banza Manteka convert (and the only one then), gave earnest exhortations to various little groups of the people both before and after the address. The people subsequently dispersed, and soon after the three missionaries and the two converts met in a room for united prayer to God for the rain; and while the last prayer was being offered down it came, fulfilling that promise, "While they are yet speaking I will hear."

As at Palabala however, that night the people drummed and danced in honour of the rain fetish, and it was long before another shower fell in that district.

In pondering these cases, it should be remembered that this drought came on in the *wet season*, when it usually rains at least every other day; that at Palabala two months preceded and one month followed the two showers of rain there, while at Banza Manteka three months preceded and one month followed; and, above all, it should be noted that the two showers in three months' drought and the one shower during four months' drought came *at the time that special prayer was made for rain.*

But what was the spiritual outcome? At the time perhaps nothing more than to lead the people from indifference to the gospel to curiosity with regard to it. But that was a great gain!

The stage of opposition to the work is a most hopeful one, for when the natives oppose, it is a sign that they are conscious of the power of the word preached, and dread its effect upon them should they continue to listen to it. As the harpooned whale rushes away from its intending captors and dives to the bottom of the sea, so at first the native under conviction of sin will go farther and farther away from the truth and sink deeper than ever into iniquity; until at last, wearied of self and of sin, he gives up his struggling, and yields himself to the Lord.

The opposition of the chiefs is usually of an insidious character. As at Palabala they will sometimes pretend to be very desirous for the people to attend the preaching, but in reality will give them secretly to understand, that it is only those specially permitted who may attend the meetings.

At Mukimbungu however, where the first converts were baptized, the opposition has always been strong, and quite open, amounting at times to positive persecution.

On one occasion when I passed through Mukimbungu, I found the brethren discussing what they should do in the event of the station being attacked. It appeared that the native chiefs had been raging against the converts, had actually put some of them to death, and had declared that on the following Sunday they would burn down the mission station and kill the missionaries. The ferocious character of these chiefs made it appear to be something more than an idle threat. However they were not allowed to do the Lord's servants any harm ; for Sunday passed by, and many another day, without anything more being heard of such an attack.

The chiefs have seldom been known to kill the converts *ostensibly on account of their religion*, but they usually effect their purpose by a charge of witchcraft. Any one who displeases the chief, or who may be disliked in the town, is in danger of being got rid of in this way. One young man, an earnest Christian, lost all his relatives in this way in a comparatively short time, and himself only escaped the same fate by removing to another district.

A noble instance of self-sacrifice occurred at Mukimbungu. Two sisters were very constant in their attendance of the meetings, and were hated by the heathen in consequence. At length the elder was accused of witchcraft, and had to take the poison water. She was a very weakly woman, and the probability was that she would not survive the ordeal, whether she vomited it (and thus established her innocence) or not. Knowing this, her younger sister came forward, and asked to be allowed to drink it instead of her sister. This, after some demur, was permitted. She drank, and vomited it; but, alas! it did not save either of them, for on some slight

"THE NATIVES SEEMED EXCITED."

pretext they were both afterwards killed! Cruel, cruel heathenism!

On some rare occasions the missionaries' lives have been threatened when they have gone to a town to preach, especially at Mukimbungu. Mr. Westlind went on one occasion to one of the towns there, taking with him several converts to give their testimony. As soon as they entered the place they saw

MR. WESTLIND,

Of Mukimbungu, Swedish Mission Station on the Congo.

something was wrong, for the people were running in every direction for their guns, and the chief made his appearance fully armed, and used very threatening language. The converts became excited, and a collision seemed imminent, when Mr. Westlind called out to the chief to know what was the matter. He replied, " I will not have you preach in my town ; if you do, I will kill you."

Mr. Westlind at once replied that he was told in God's book not to force people to hear if they did not wish, but to go away and leave them, shaking the very dust off from their feet as a testimony against them. " The next time I come will be when you send for me," said Mr. Westlind, and he left them. When I passed through Mukimbungu some little time after this, these people were debating among themselves, whether they should not send for the white man, to visit them once more.

As stated before, it was at Mukimbungu that the first baptisms on the Congo took place. It would not be easy for us to forget the memorable day of the simple but most significant ceremony. The baptism of those first five converts from heathenism was a cause of joy, not only because of their individual deliverance from the bondage of darkness, but also because they were regarded as firstfruits, after the long years of toil,—firstfruits to Christ from Congoland.

It was a day we had longed and prayed for, while yet it seemed to be distant. We knew a blessing would come, but not whether *we* should be permitted to witness it, or only our successors, when we were gone for ever. But now it was come!

How would the dear pioneers who sleep in Jesus have rejoiced to see that day—Telford and Petersen, Lanceley and McCall, and others! Was it certain they were *not* present with us? At least they rejoiced, for there was joy in the presence of the angels of God over these penitent sinners, as they turned from their devil worship to God, and publicly confessed their faith in the gospel.

It seemed to us the dawn of a new epoch! Henceforth the conversion of multitudes of the heathen would be only a question of time! The seed had begun to germinate, there would in due season be a crop. Each of these converts would be a missionary, and all converted through *them* would in turn become missionaries too! How much easier would be the work in time to come, when each white missionary might be assisted by earnest *native* evangelists, men of the same colour and language as the people themselves! The heathen could not *then* regard the gospel as exclusively the white man's religion. In the salvation of these five converts from heathenism we had the earnest of Congo for Christ, and saw a marvellous work *begun!* We praised God for what we believed He was *going to do*, as well as for the glad sight which our eyes witnessed.

Within twelve months of this time a great awakening took place in the district of BANZA MANTEKA. Mr. Henry Richards, who had founded the mission there, and had been sowing the good seed for years

MR. HENRY RICHARDS,
OF BANZA MANTEKA.

AN IMPORTANT STEP IN ADVANCE. 57

with no slack hand, noticed a special interest in the word preached. The arm of the Lord had awoke. He was conscious that the Spirit of the Lord, in answer to much prayer, was upon him, to preach the gospel in such a way and with such success as he had not before seen in Africa. One reason for the change was possibly that his greater familiarity with the language enabled him to use it more freely and forcibly, and his more perfect knowledge of Congo life put him in a position to employ *Congo illustrations*, as windows to let the light in. He saw that in proportion as he did this his meaning was grasped, and his teachings felt as they had not previously been.

When he went into the towns to preach, large numbers came to listen, and often when he had finished an address of an hour or an hour and a half in length, they would ask him not to go away, but tell them more. The interest increased and spread, until the people almost besieged the station; from outlying districts they came also, bringing provisions, that they might stay and hear the word of God constantly. From morning till night Mr. Richards was engaged in preaching, teaching, and examining converts; and this went on for weeks. So busy was he that he often had not opportunity even to eat. He contented himself with two daily meals, reluctant to spare time for a third.

The conversions which took place seemed to be sound and satisfactory. A son of the old king Makokila was one of the first, and this greatly displeased the nephew of the king, who, according to Fiote custom, would succeed the chief when he died.

"Whatever is the matter with you?" he said very angrily; "I can't make it out"; and he went down to the meeting in the evening in a great rage, intending by his presence to prevent any more conversions. But the Spirit of God convinced him so powerfully of sin, that he too had to plead for mercy there and then, and soon found peace in believing in Jesus. The king's son was delighted, but could not help rallying him a little, saying in his turn, "Well, and whatever is the matter with *you?*" "Oh!" replied he "I *am* so happy! I understand it all now."

Soon after this the gray-haired old chief himself (Makokila) surrendered his heart to God, and became a humble follower of the Lord Jesus; for the power of the Lord was present to heal, even in very obstinate cases.

One man had been exceptionally vile. He was a "medicine man," and had been a great deceiver of the people. Clearly stamped upon his face were the marks of the villain. He openly opposed the gospel, and tried to persuade the people not to listen to it, and often when Mr. Richards passed by him, on his way to preach, this man would spit after him in contempt, and curse him horribly.

When I was visiting Banza Manteka, soon after the revival had begun, I saw this man on the path coming towards me. I knew him very well by sight, and said to myself, "Can this be the same man?"

Tom, one of the Christian lads of the Mission, wearing the head-dress of a Congo witch-doctor.

He hastened towards me, his face aglow with a light not of earth. From being one of the ugliest old men I ever saw, he had so changed as to be positively beautiful. Formerly he might have sat for one of

Doré's demons; but now the peace of God that passeth all understanding lit up his countenance, and joy in the Holy Ghost made it radiant. He seemed to have saved body as well as soul, and I marvelled at the power of the grace which had transformed him.

And not only men, but women and boys and girls in considerable numbers were brought under great concern for their souls. It was pitiable to hear the confessions that were made from time to time by mere lads, showing how old in vice they had already become! Strange to say, some *young children* gave the clearest and brightest testimony of having received salvation.

One day a woman brought a very little girl to be examined as a candidate for baptism. Mr. Richards and I were surprised that one so young (she could not have been more than six or seven) should be brought as a candidate.

"Do you think she understands?" asked Mr. Richards. "Try her," said the mother quite confidently; and we both plied her with questions, and were astonished at her answers. How wonderful it was! Only a few days before both mother and child were in heathen darkness and ignorance; *now* a wonderful wisdom was given to this poor little lamb! Some of the worldly-wise might have sat at her feet and learned lessons of priceless value. We said to each other in amazement, "This is the doing of God! He is revealing His truth to babes—heathen babes!"

We commended the woman for endeavouring to

BANZA MANTEKA CHRISTIANS. 61

take her. children with her to heaven. She looked radiantly happy, and said, " Not only this one, but you also" (apostrophising an infant at her breast), "you also will give your heart to Jesus when you are old enough to know, won't you ? "

Much care had however to be exercised in the receiving of candidates for baptism. Mr. Richards felt the responsibility to be very great. He knew how easy it was to be deceived by those who were really in earnest, but who were perhaps at the same time to some extent self-deceived.

He decided to baptize at first only those of whom he was thoroughly confident, and of these to form a small Church. Afterwards they would help in the decision of the cases of other candidates, at least to the extent of judging of their outward conduct. This plan has been found to answer remarkably well, and it is the practice followed at each of the stations. No foreigner can know a native as well as a fellow native can. Their knowledge of each other is almost complete, as even domestic life is lived quite openly, and there is no such thing as reserve or privacy.

This carefulness in receiving candidates for baptism has made the Church growth slow. The Banza Manteka Church numbers now only a little over two hundred *baptized* believers, though the number of converts is much larger. At Mukimbungu, Lukungu, and Palabala there are also smaller Churches, bringing the number of baptized members to above five hundred. It might have been double this, but purity and future usefulness have been sought rather than numbers, and rightly so.

It will be asked, Of what quality are these converts? Do they stand well? Are they zealous for God? Do they provoke one another to love and good works? The answer is cheering.

There have up to the present been wonderfully few cases of backsliding or falling into open sin. The Churches in this respect will compare very favourably with average European or American Churches.

The converts are also self-denying and zealous. They will go away for days from their homes and families to take the gospel to outlying districts, without any fee or reward, and entirely at their own charges.

Some little time ago Dr. Gordon's Church, of Boston, Mass., U.S.A., gave an iron building capable of holding six hundred people to the Banza Manteka Church, on the condition that the members of the Church would carry it from the lower river. This they have done *by a great amount of self-sacrificing toil.* The loads numbered about seven or eight hundred, and some of them were very heavy. The able-bodied men of the Church went down five or six times to Underhill, a distance of *fifty-five miles*, and brought back on their heads each time loads of at least sixty pounds weight! The women and children of course were not able to do this, so they worked in their fields, sold their surplus stock of vegetables, and with the cloth gained they engaged other men to go and share in the transport on their behalf. The average value of the labour that each of these converts gave thus to the Lord would be between three and four pounds, no small contribution from poor native Congoese!

The converts as a rule are simple-minded and single-hearted. They sincerely love their Lord, and try heartily to obey Him. The contrast between their former heathen state and their present condition is so great, that they are constantly full of wonder and gratitude to God. They are not troubled with doubts and fears, but rely with the simplicity of children on the sweet promises of their Father God.

One of the chiefs in a district near Lukungu (where there is a Church of believers) became converted through a man who was our cook for about twelve months. He had himself been led to Christ during the stir that took place at Lukungu on the news of the awakening at Banza Manteka. The cook spoke to his chief about his soul and about the Saviour, creating an interest which brought him soon afterwards as an inquirer to the station, and resulted in his becoming a decided Christian. This chief in turn has been the means of the conversion of several others in his own town. He is, thank God! a burning and shining light wherever he goes. He endeavours to live out the Lord's command, " As ye go, preach," for he is notorious as one " instant in season, out of season " in testifying for the Lord.

A short time ago I received a letter from one of the converted lads, telling me of a remarkable circumstance that had just happened in this man's town. His child was very sick, and it seemed to be unto death. Mayala, the chief, being much concerned, went to the mission station and procured medicine for him, and administered it, but without any satisfactory result. At last some of his people came to him, and begged him to take the child to the fetish house, but he refused. Still the child did not get better, but rather grew worse. At length the people fetched the medicine-man, but Mayala positively declined to allow him to interfere with his child, saying that he believed in the power of God. The people somewhat derisively replied, " We should like to see this power of God!" *"You shall see it,"* responded Mayala. So entering his hut, he shut to the door, and prayed, and his " Father which seeth in secret," rewarded him openly.

The sick child was outside the house under the verandah, and while his father was in the hut praying for him, he fell into a deep sleep. Still the father wrestled with God in prayer for his child, and the people gathered round in curious wonderment. At last Mayala received the assurance he wanted, and he went outside his hut to the people. They were all expectation, *and so was he;* and God, who has promised that "the prayer of faith shall save the sick," raised the child up. He awoke, got up, *and was soon playing about as if nothing had been the matter with him.*

Who taught Mayala this "healing by faith"? The Holy Spirit of God. No one had taught him the *doctrine.* It was his own childlike interpretation of such promises as "what things soever ye desire when ye pray, believe that ye receive them, and ye shall have them." They led him to take his child's case to the Lord Himself, instead of to the medicine-man; and the more so as he had already been to the disciples, and they could not render him any help. He felt too that the very existence of Divine power had been challenged, and he asked God to show forth that power in the sight of the people.

Sometimes when I have seen such men as these living earnest, consecrated lives, and walking by simple faith, I have thought: "Shall what the Lord has prophesied indeed come to pass, that the last shall be first, that the poor, dark, downtrodden Africans shall yet be called into the kingdom of grace, and through their child-like and whole-hearted reception of God's eternal truth become bright illustrations of faith and devotion, in these last days of scoffing unbelief and Laodicean selfishness?"

C. R.

MR. JOHN McKITTRICK, OF BELFAST,
Leader of the Congo-Balolo Mission.

CHAPTER V.

A WALK IN BALOLOLAND.

Recollections by Mr. J. McKittrick.

For several months after reaching Wangata I waited in vain a favourable opportunity to visit a district said to be large and populous, twenty miles east of our mission station. The people told me of "big towns" up the Juapa, Ikelemba, and Lulonga rivers, and of Welu, a "strong chief," residing at a place called Bonsole. They would also often tell me of the land from which their fathers came, saying with an air of pride, "We are few and weak here," meaning on the banks of the Congo between Wangata and Ikengo; "but we are very many and very strong away yonder," pointing southward.

Wishing to know more of the Balolo, I decided to visit Bonsole, and made arrangements to have our canoe cleaned and prepared for the trip. Whilst Bojuela was engaged in making ready the canoe, I went to see how he was getting on. A man came to the landing stage and asked where the white man was going; returning, he told his townsfolk, most of whom came out a few minutes later to hear the news.

"Where are you going, Bondele?" inquired a

spokesman of the people, a good-natured fellow called Ngolo, observing the preparations.

"To Bonsole," I replied.

"All right, Bondele; if you bring your rifle, and agree to fight with the Boluke, we'll go with you; but if not, we won't," said Ngolo frankly.

"I'll take my rifle, but I can't fight; you know that I am a man of peace," I replied decidedly.

"We know you are a coward, Bondele!" said he laughing; "so we won't go by water. But we'll go overland with you if you like, and carry your things for you."

"All right; that will do just as well. We will get off to-morrow morning."

They occupied themselves the rest of the day in making ready, and next morning we started. Taking the Inganda road, which led us through a large district of the same name, and keeping down the right bank of the Congo for about five miles, we soon turned off into the Bonsole and Bolenge track.

I was pleasantly surprised at the size of the towns and the number of their inhabitants in the prosperous district through which we walked, and could not help saying to myself, "Here I have lived at Wangata all these months ignorant of the thousands of this highly favoured Inganda!" But till one has more or less of the language, even local exploration is difficult. We wended our way over elevated land, through large plantations and clearings, covering a vast tract of country, which must have taken many years to reclaim from the virgin forest and bring under cul-

GAME AND WILDFOWL ON AN AFRICAN RIVER.

FOREST COVERED BANKS OF THE CONGO.

tivation. Then we descended into a dense wooded swamp, where I had to divest myself of boots and socks, and splash through water and mud; several heavy tornadoes, a day or two before, having so flooded the road that in some places the water was knee deep. Yet even here, strange to say, though the trees grow thick and tall, with innumerable creepers and thick underbush between, I perceived none of the offensive malarious odour, so common in the thickets of the Lower Congo.

Swampy valleys like this alternated with ridges throughout our twenty-mile walk. We were going south, so the watery vales we kept crossing ran parallel to the Congo, and some of them were of sufficient depth to form tortuous channels of water.

According to native report, one of these channels leads from the Juapa River to Lake Matumba, and by it the Boluke traders are said to go down to Irebu and Ngombe, when there is war in the neighbourhood of, or at the mouth of the Juapa. I have little doubt that such a channel exists, and if so Wangata is built on a great island, and not on the mainland.

About noon we reached a town called Bompafu, an outlying portion of Inganda, where resides an old and influential chief. We did not halt here, but, seeing the old man as we passed, my men saluted him, bowing almost to the ground, and clapping their hands as they cried out, " *Wandou!* " " Hail, king ! "

On again through the forest after a lunch of dried fish and cassava. About four in the afternoon we reached the outskirts of Bonsole, where I found the main entrance to the place barricaded and carefully guarded by a few watchmen. The barricade, which consisted of the end of a house placed across the entrance and secured to a number of upright poles, was owing to hostilities with the people of another

YALULINA NATIVES.

district, which were fortunately suspended for the time. An aperture in the end of the house thus placed in the road was the only entrance, and by no means an easy one, measuring about three feet by one and a half.

After exchanging presents with an elder, we walked through the town. The people were very civil; the children flocked out to see the white man; the little fellows would run past me, and then wait in the path to take a good look at my white face as I came forward, and then hastily scamper off. I do not know that I have seen finer or more lively boys, bright, smiling, well fed, and clean, just what all lads should be! It was near sun-down when we reached Welu's residence. He was absent when I arrived; but his son hastened to give me a kind welcome, and to show me the hut in which I was to stay. Here I was glad to rest my weary limbs; but, alas! it was not for long. Young Welu soon came to say that it was a custom among them that strangers should sit outside, so that all the people may have an opportunity of looking at them. Yielding to his persuasive eloquence, I went out, and took up my seat beneath the palms, and resignedly made myself a public gazing stock for fifteen or twenty minutes.

I then learned that I was to receive a present from the king, and was of course expected to make a handsome one in return. For this I was prepared. After taking a little food accordingly, I was summoned forth once more, but this time to a very formal and imposing audience, for which elaborate preparations in the way of hair-dressing

"ELABORATE PREPARATIONS IN THE WAY OF HAIR-DRESSING."

and personal decoration had evidently been made. I was seated in the midst of a large, representative assembly of men and women, which had been summoned by drum. A goat was brought (bound), and laid at my feet; fowls, palm nuts, plaintains, and a dish out of which to take food were also given. Welu made an effective speech. When it was over I produced my "dash,"—a brass helmet and a piece of savelist. Welu looked gloomy! I then produced some beads and cowries, some spoons and forks, and a plate; and forthwith the cloud was replaced by the broad grin of satisfaction, so often seen on similar occasions on the countenances of these "children of a larger growth" in Central Africa!

Strolling later on through the town, I was told that in one quarter of it there resided a white woman just like myself! On reaching the place, I saw an albino with a child in her arms. "Is she not white?" said they; "like the Englese wo talu-tale" (the Englishman of length, a name by which they called me owing to my stature).

She was an unnatural looking creature, like neither African nor European, with light complexion, red eyes, and a peculiar expression of face. She did not enjoy being likened to the white man, and soon retreated into a house.

I had my accordion with me, and it quickly gathered a crowd. Seating myself on a log of wood, I played a few hymn-tunes. Our boys who were with me would sometimes sing the hymns, but on this occasion the little fellows were shy. An old dame called out to her little grandchild in the crowd "Come away! come away from the spirit!" Some of the men laughed, but some looked serious. It would never do to have the story that I was "a spirit" go abroad, as it would block my way everywhere. But how disprove the assertion? I pulled up my jacket, unbuttoned my shirt sleeve and bared my arm. Then extending it I said: "Feel that! is it not flesh and bone? A spirit has not these!" A laugh against the old lady went round, and the people were re-assured. It was hard to get away from them.

On my way back I was stopped at the house of an old chief, and entreated to begin again to play the instrument. The kind women had ready for me on our return such an abundance of dainty dishes of their own preparation, that I had an *embarras de richesses*. Matron after matron arrived, each bearing a vessel carefully covered with a plantain leaf, bound on with a cord, to exclude dust and insects. There was food enough for a week and to spare. What was I to do? My men, seeing such a superabundance of "chop," volunteered their services, and I was saved all further trouble! The vessels were speedily ready to be returned to their owners.

As I was anxious to see the whole district, I started again the following morning, accompanied by Bojuela and one or two of our schoolboys, in the opposite direction. Our way led, for the most part, through a succession of villages, without any protection from the sun. By the time we reached the extreme end of the "town" our clothes were tolerably well saturated!

The villages of this part of the country are situated on a high ridge of land. The soil, which in the forests is of deep alluvium, is exceedingly rich and fertile, as seen by the luxuriant abundance that everywhere meets the eye. Food is much cheaper hereabouts than at Wangata, for the people attend more to agriculture than do those nearer the river. Maize and mandioca are the principal crops, and flourish everywhere. Much attention is given to the cultivation of the sugar cane, which grows to an extraordinary height and thickness, and is exceedingly sweet and juicy. Large patches of it are met with near the towns for convenience, the other fields being as a rule farther removed from the dwellings.

Even the old people are not without a local industry; they engage in grinding camwood, which is carefully prepared and forwarded to Ikango, Inganda, and other places, whence it is taken by native merchants to tribes as far down the river as Stanley Pool. This wood is found in great abundance in the forests of the interior, and when ground into powder and prepared, is used for dyeing purposes; it imparts a rich and beautiful crimson. It is used by the natives as a cosmetic also.

On the whole, the people in this neighbourhood seemed more superstitious than their neighbours, and less kindly disposed towards Europeans. This may have arisen from the losses that they had sustained from their recent battle with the Bandaka. One of the deceased warriors had been a man of considerable standing in his town, so they were about to have a human sacrifice at his funeral. But the chief, whose guest I was, brought the matter before his counsellors, and it was decided to postpone the ceremony till I was gone; for, said he, "the white man does not like to hear of people being killed." The victim was marked out and possibly bound; but the execution, which they carry out with terrible barbarity, was postponed in deference to me, an illustration of the effect of the mere presence of a white man among these people.

On reaching what is called the *ntundu*, or the end of the village, I was led a little way beyond the houses to a high palisade, which—securely fastened and carefully guarded at night—is used as a sort of citadel in case of attack. The people soon flocked round me; but, oh! how miserable they seemed when compared with the inhabitants of other villages! how timid and fearful!

In Africa the state of uncertainty and insecurity created by war ruins a village very quickly. Owing to the frail nature of the houses, from the perishable building material used, decay sets in immediately, unless the buildings are kept in constant repair. Dilapidated houses, and others fast falling into ruin, meet the eye on all sides in this unhappy place.

To the best of my ability I tried to tell them of the Friend and Saviour of sinners. They seemed interested, the story was new to them. It was the first and only occasion on which they heard the name of Jesus, but the gospel which Christ committed to His disciples will, please God, before long overthrow all their superstitions, and save them from their sins and sorrows! Such is our hope and expectation.

On our way back I stopped at a place where a goodly number of leading men had assembled to discuss a question, which, judging from the numbers present, must have been of some considerable importance. They were seated in a quiet spot by the wayside under the shade of a few friendly banana trees. Most of them were well armed, as is usual in this part of the interior, where all men when travelling are armed to the teeth. I was again called upon to "*kunda n'sauge*," play the instrument; and taking my seat in the midst of the wise men of Bonsole, I succeeded in interesting them for a considerable time. One big fellow was captivated with the music, and insisted on handling the accordion for himself, to see that there was nothing supernatural about it.

We inspected afterwards several of the troughs in which the sugarcane is reduced to a pulp. The trough is divided into two parts, the smaller is narrow at the bottom, and in this the sugarcane is pounded; the other is much larger, and as wide at the bottom as at the top. In this the cane is steeped for some time before pressing and straining into huge earthen jars, in which it is carefully covered up. The remains of the woody substance create fermentation, and in a few days it is ready for use. When fresh it is a pleasant and wholesome drink, and not intoxicating.

Farther on we came to a part of the village which had evidently once been more thickly populated. On the site of a house there were heaped up a number of

a N'GUMA-BAYANSI.
b NATIVE OF URINDI.
c TYPE OF MABUNGU.
d, d MEN SMOKING ELAND-HORN PIPES.

earthenware vessels. They looked red, as if the house had been burned over them. A solitary and large hut stood near; in front of it, on the other side of the street, was a pole about three feet high, with a human skull of extraordinary size on the top.

The earthenware, the burned hut, the skull, and the deserted appearance of the place, all combined to tell the sorrowful tale. The chief had been carried off by death, and the skull on the pole was that of the poor victim who had been sacrificed at his funeral. These human sacrifices used to be of frequent occurrence at Wangata, but are now forbidden by the Congo Free State. They are continued still, however, at Inganda, and all over the interior.

My men were by this time anxious to start homewards, and though Welu would fain have detained us longer, I thought it best to leave the interesting, good-natured people of Bonsole. I had proved that a missionary would be welcomed in that district, and that the people would even be proud to entertain him. I had learned that the banks of the great river are by no means the most populous or desirable locality for mission stations, though in some respects the most convenient. But they give access to the great interior, and oh the immensity of that field!

My men got the start of me, and at a forest village on the outskirts of the Bonsole district were stopped by an attempt of the local chief to levy blackmail. But even in these wild regions there is a measure of law, and this man Eanga knew that he, in trying to demand a price for permission to pass, was breaking native law. It was only a fowl he wanted; but without this tax he would not let my man carrying the goat pass. I resolved not to pay what was an unfair demand; so leaving the goat and all the rest of Welu's presents, I ordered him to carry them back to the chief and explain.

We had not got far on our way before, first young Welu and then his father, came up breathless, angry, excited, apologising for the insult, and threatening that unless I would overlook it and take the present with me, Eanga and all his must perish! Of course we yielded, obtaining a promise that no harm should come to the culprit.

After parting from Welu, we continued for some time crossing densely wooded high land, but then gradually descended inwards to a forest swamp—a "dismal swamp" indeed! The path was thick with mud and dead vegetation; we felt the slippery network of roots underneath, making the road most difficult, while stately forest monarchs towered high overhead, creating a perpetual semi-darkness. Young trees and bushes strove for the mastery below, and owing to the thickness of the foliage the sun's rays scarcely ever penetrate this grim solitude. Here the eagle, the hawk, and other large birds make their homes, and their voices alone, as they are roused by the footsteps of the traveller, disturb the stillness. The place is such that the leopard could scarcely make his lair in it, as the ground is for the most part under water. We were thankful to emerge on drier ground.

As we approached Wangata, the men tried, before entering the town, to make themselves as neat and clean as circumstances would permit. I resolved to pass the night at the house of an old chief, whom I had met on a former occasion at our station. He seemed somewhat disconcerted by my arrival at first, and proposed giving me very poor accommodation for the night—an old cook house, which, though it had a good roof, boasted no walls. Telling my men to have my things placed inside, I sat down among the people; but my two confidential friends, Boyela and Eakola, soon came and whispered, " White man, these people are thieves, and if you stay in this place you will lose your things."

"Well," I replied, "the chief told me to stay in it. You had better tell him that if anything is stolen I shall hold him responsible."

He soon returned and said, " Come along, Bondele; you shall stay in another house," and I was pleased to find that a room in the chief's own house had been appointed for me. His residence consisted of three rooms, one of which was occupied by the mother and little ones, the other one by the father and older members of the family, whilst the centre apartment was appointed for me.

When it grew dark bright fires were lighted outside,

the surroundings were illuminated by bonfires, and a torch of gum-copal, which had been placed in the centre, served as a flambeau. The people all engaged in the dance, and one of my men was the leading spirit of the revel, his song could be heard above all the rest. I was watching them, and overheard one of the onlookers say to his fellow in the crowd, "How is it that this man is not afraid? he is only one white man among so many!" It was the very town where Bolesi the slave, whom I had ransomed five or six months before, had been so cruelly treated; but I was about my Master's business, and feared no evil.

Giving my host a fathom of cloth in return for his kindness, we were starting early next morning, when to my surprise several of the principal men grouped themselves on the street in front of us. They appeared anxious to make a lasting friendship, and insisted on my accepting a present of three or four goats. I told them I had nothing in the shape of a return present, and therefore could not take their gift; but as they insisted, I arranged that they should bring their presents to Wangata, which they did most willingly.

This place is called Upper Wangata, and must contain I think not less than two thousand inhabitants. The houses are oblong in shape, fairly and well built and arranged on either side of the street in admirable order. The country between this town and the Congo is not swampy, but covered with a dense forest. Half a day's brisk march brought us to our own station.

The cannibalism of the Balolo is not quite so revolting as that described on the Mobangi, and in other parts of the Congo Free State. As far as I was able to observe or ascertain, human flesh is not bought and eaten merely for food. It *is* eaten, but mainly as a superstitious rite connected with funerals.

When an old chief thinks his end draws nigh, he calls together his family relations and slaves, appoints the disposition of his wives and property, and mentions the slaves who are to be slain at his interment. As each name is called aloud, the destined victim of superstition replies, " N'ko joi " (I care not). Then addressing himself to his nearest relation, the old man, striking one hand on the other, adjures them to carry out this last injunction, saying, " If these die not, may ye all die ! "

Such is the force of custom and the cruelty of superstition, that the poor, ignorant people feel as if they had no voice. The murders *must* follow the death.

As soon as the old man is gone, and before any death wail is raised, a quiet search is made for the foredoomed men or women, who are bound fast in a place of safety and starved till the day of execution, the mode of which we have described elsewhere. The body of the victim is at once divided, cooked, and eaten. The head is taken down from the tree, soaked till the skull is cleaned of flesh, and stuck up on a pole before the dead man's house.

In the case of great chiefs, children are killed and buried in the grave. The Balolo are in this respect

CANNIBALISM.

fearfully cruel. The boys are stuffed with food, especially prepared by the relations of the late chief, and led forth to the slaughter. Strong creepers like ropes from the forest are secured round their necks. A man climbs a tree; when high enough he seeks a firm foothold, and then raises the victim from the

ground—higher and higher, till the rope is suddenly let go and the child killed by the fall, or *not* killed, as the case may be. If not, the mangled victim is brutally beaten to death!

It would be considered a proof of the utmost disrespect to omit these horrible customs; the family doing so would lose all social standing, and become the jest of the community.

Conceive it if you can, English Christians! All through the towns and villages of the ten millions of Balolo, these horrors are being continually enacted, and worse horrors still in many parts of the Congo Free State. Death is bad enough anywhere; but death in Congoland when the deceased is above the rank of slave is invariably followed by murder, and often by many murders. Tens of thousands of such murders must take place each year. The law forbidding them in the Congo Free State can be enforced —as yet—at comparatively few points only.

Observing grown men suddenly hiding themselves behind trees, under bushes, or otherwise, without any apparent reason, I one day inquired the cause, and found it was because the man's mother-in-law had come in sight. "But why should a big man hide away from a woman?" I asked. "O Bondele! he *ashamed!*" "Ashamed! of what?" "He *afraid* too!" "Afraid! how so?" Then I learned that for a man to face his mother-in-law is esteemed a breach of the Balolo laws of marriage, and that a woman so insulted would bring a charge against her son-in-law before the elders of the town, who would inflict heavy damages! "Bondele," said Bompole to me one day, soon after his arrival at Harley House, "doctor's mother-in-law come here, he run away?" "No, my boy, no!" said I, laughing at the idea. "Oh! you no do so?" he replied gravely; then catching the fun of the notion, he laughed too. But many of our customs seemed as strange to him as Balolo usages had done to me.

Unless for a very serious offence a husband does not put away his wife, if she is a free woman. Her friends possess the dowry or price he paid for her, and unless he can get that back he will not part with her! If she wishes to leave her husband, and her relations consent, the dowry is returned, and she is free. Even in the case of a slave wife—one bought with

money, not betrothed with dowry—the husband cannot, without some grave charge against her, sell her again. The elders of the town expostulate, if they hear he has any desire to do so, try to moderate his displeasure, and show that she is really valuable to him. He may not be persuaded, but few care to oppose the chief men of the district, and thus many disputes and misunderstandings are settled without separation.

The Balolo quite understand family life, and the

women are really industrious and domestic. Their daily life is simple and natural. The wives and children start early for the fields or gardens, often at a distance from the village, and work diligently till noon, clearing, weeding, hoeing, planting, or reaping, as the case may be. At noon they take a mid-day meal, and rest, resuming toil afterwards. Towards evening they return to their houses, carrying large bundles of firewood, should there be a scarcity round the village, and then they prepare the evening meal.

Unlike the people on the Lower Congo, each father takes his seat in the centre of the family group of wives and children, frequently with the youngest child on his knee, and he divides the fish or meat, while the wives distribute the other food. I have often shared such pleasant evening meals with Balolo families.

CHAPTER VI.

A CHAT WITH MR. RICHARDS, OF BANZA MANTEKA.

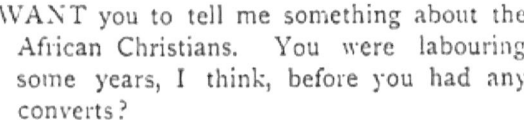

I WANT you to tell me something about the African Christians. You were labouring some years, I think, before you had any converts?

Yes; six years more or less! Of course I had at first to build and plant and get acclimatized. Then I had to learn the language—no easy task when you have no teacher and no books. It was years before I could understand and enjoy hearing it, and before I could use it with any power.

Yes, of course! And you had illnesses and deep sorrows?

I had. God blessed them to me. On my first visit to England on account of health I was greatly exercised about the apparent lack of blessing in Africa. I felt I must be blessed if I was to be made a blessing. And when I got back my one desire was for converts. A great yearning for souls took possession of me. I could not sleep for it sometimes, and had to pray God to take it away, for it was consuming me. But there was no sign of blessing. I resolved to go elsewhere if the word bore no fruit at Banza Manteka. But first I asked myself what was the fault? I was preaching the truth, and the people listened; but they did not seem to *feel* in the least.

Yet you were in earnest, were you not?

Dead in earnest! But as I read I began to see I had been

trying the wrong way to do good to the heathen. I had been much occupied with many things, and the one great thing to which a missionary should devote himself mainly, if not exclusively, *preaching*, had not been made prominent enough. It is so easy in Congo to get distracted. There is so much to do. Building, planting, ordinary business of various sorts, learning the language, teaching, writing, travelling,—all these things are apt to squeeze the preaching into a corner.

I can easily understand that! Congo is like England in that respect.

Ay! but the consequences are more serious there. Preaching —" the foolishness of preaching"—is God's one great ordinance for the salvation of men. When the revival came I was no longer satisfied with occasional services and regular Sunday work. I gave myself to preaching daily—twice a day. One year I preached seven hundred times. And the people don't care for short sermons. They like a full hour or hour and a half. They have so much to learn.

But surely people could never attend so many and such long meetings?

Ah! but they *do*. I asked them to choose their own time. They fixed one o'clock, when all their field work is done and they have had their mid-day meal. And again, later in the evening, they come freely and eagerly. But they like to hear the *same* teacher. Changes put them out very much, for they do not gain confidence all at once. They want the same voice, and the same thing taught over and over again. They learn only from the preacher, at first at any rate; not, as here, from books and from intercourse. The preaching consequently should be daily, and, if possible, two or three times a·day. Weekly preaching is no use; it is all forgotten before the next service.

But a missionary must do other things. He must teach the school, for instance.

No! that is mere waste of time *at first*. When the people are converted, *then* have schools for the Christians, that they may learn to read the word of God and teach it in their turn But preaching with a view to conversion, immediate conversion, this is God's commandment, and this is the missionary's work—his prime, principal, paramount, peculiar duty. If you want schools, send out teachers; but missionaries go to make converts.

But when people are converted they need teaching?

Undoubtedly. That is the object of our incessant meetings. We have to teach them to observe all things that Christ has commanded; and I assure you it takes a lot of teaching to do that among the Congoese! We want to get the converts ready to be in their turn teachers and preachers as quickly as possible. As regards the Christians, it is teach, teach, teach, all the time. They soon learn more than you would think. The Spirit of God seems to make them intelligent. They learn to read fast; they open little schools in other villages to teach their own townsfolk to do the same. They send their children to school too fast enough *as soon as they are converted*—though before we had actually to ransom slave children in order to get a school at all. The *heathen* want to be paid for coming to school.

Yes! conversion makes all the difference. What truths did you find most fitted to awaken attention and touch the heart?

Ah! that is the core and kernel of the whole thing. I went to work the wrong way at first. My first idea was to teach the heathen the folly of idolatry and superstition, the nature of God, about His will as expressed in the law, about duty and morality and such things, as well as about Christ, His words, His miracles, and parables, His death and resurrection. But I found it all no use. At the end of six years I had not a convert.

Well?

Then in bitterness of spirit I prayed and searched the Scriptures, and noted what the apostles did, and began to follow their example.

But surely they did all the things you just named.

Afterwards! But they did something else *first*. They preached Christ and Him crucified; they made people feel their guilt in killing and rejecting Him, in not resembling Him, in not caring for and coming to Him. They kept to the one point, and Christ Himself bade them do so. They were to proclaim repentance and remission of sins through Him! Not a hundred things. One thing—Christ and Him crucified.

Yes, and you were trying to lead up to that, to prepare the people to appreciate the gospel.

Ay! But when I gave up all leading to it, and preached *that*, day by day and week by week, then I speedily saw a glorious change! Then I had proof that Paul was right, when he said that it is the gospel itself that is the power of God to salvation. I don't go into the philosophy of the thing, but I saw the facts; and I think facts are more convincing than philosophy. When once I took this ground, and charged the people with sin for not believing in Christ, and urged that He was the only Saviour, and ready to save them then and there, then I felt clothed with power, and that it was the Spirit of God who spoke through me.

And what were the results?

Heart-cheering! Marvellous! The stolid, stupid people waked up. I saw looks and whispers, and nudges between neighbours, astonishment, eager interest, and soon conviction and shame, tears of penitence; restless desire to hear, more shame, alarm, and very soon I was assailed on all sides with the question, "What must I do to be saved?" I was alone most of the time, and positively I had no time, no, not so much as to eat some days. The whole place and the country-side was in a stir. I had to neglect all else; I was preaching, and dealing with inquirers all day long. And soon the converts were numbered by hundreds.

What proof had you they were real converts, that the movement was not one of mere excitement?

Every proof I could desire, or that you would desire here. The people loved Christ and obeyed Him. They began to love their Bibles, or rather such portions of Scripture as they had. They cared for nothing compared to worship and prayer. They began to bear witness for Christ among their people. They cheerfully endured persecution, and risked their lives for the sake of their new faith. The thieves—and they are all thieves to begin with—became honest; the liars—and lying was customary—became truthful; the women became modest, and wanted dresses directly they were converted. I remember one who, as soon as she had received Christ and was rejoicing in Him, said to the sister who had been evangelizing her, " But now I want some clothes; I don't like having my skin outside!"

Poor dear woman! But do the Christians then dress like we do?

Oh, no! we should be very sorry to urge that. I greatly object to any attempt to Europeanise Africans. Africans they are, and Africans they must continue in all their habits and customs. But the dress of the heathen is not sufficient either for decency or comfort, and the Christians, poor as they are, invariably manage to cover themselves. The husbands do all the sewing in Congo, and Christian husbands soon make their wives a dress, or get them a cloth. The women like *dresses;* that is, garments made like a nightgown with a good deep yoke for the neck and a band, and coming down to the ankles. When we *have* such, we *give* them, but we get very few! My wife is very anxious to take back a good stock. They should be made of strong stuff like dusters, blue checked cloth which we call " domestics" and use for trade.

Do they like that better than dark prints of various colours?

Well, at present the women have not seen those, and, like ladies here, they wish to be in the fashion, not peculiar. They don't like to be looked at. If everybody wore print they would like it. If you can get us a number of dresses made, all alike, it would not much matter what sort of calico was used. Only as the women sit at times on the ground, light or white dresses would soil quickly.

What do the men wear?

Generally a cloth round the legs and waist, and a loose jacket or smockfrock, something like a shirt, outside. We often sell them shirts for the purpose. I hate to see an African in trousers! They suit us, but they spoil them! And they never keep them in good order.

Do they feel the heat as you do?

Yes, so much so that when carrying—toiling in the sun up steep hills with loads on their heads—they perspire most copiously. Then of course they divest themselves of their garments, as

CARRYING.

do the women while they work in the fields. But the mornings and evenings are chilly, and garments are a comfort. If the thermometer does not stand above 70° the people shiver and say, "How cold it is!"

Those dear converts of whom you speak,—can you love them and feel to them as you would to English fellow Christians?

Oh! precisely. *They are exactly like us inside;* the difference is only skin deep! They are intensely sincere. What is in comes out! There are no restraints of any kind—no delicacy or consideration or deference to public opinion or conventionalities, of course. A man in the audience, if he does not agree with my conclusion, or follow my explanation, will exclaim, "Oh, I don't think so," or, "I don't see that at all"; or if one is teaching any special duty, he will object, "Then why did you do so and so?" But that is a matter of custom; their hearts are just like ours.

But are they affectionate, kind, grateful, faithful to those they love, like Europeans?

That is just what *they* ask about white men! My dear wife was very ill one night; I was up with her and anxious, and I suppose I looked pale next day. Lydia, a woman who kindly came in to help, observed it, and I overheard her saying to a neighbour, "What *do* you think? These white people *actually love each other like we do!* She is ill, and he looks pale." It was evidently a new discovery to her that white folks had human feelings! I have come to the conclusion that there is little difference in reality. There is a mutual want of appreciation at first.

Well, but how treacherous and unkind they often are to white people, and how awfully cruel to each other at times, killing the innocent, burning and drowning, and selling into slavery!

True. But all that is easily accounted for. As to the missionaries, remember that they *knew white men before they knew missionaries!* It is not long since slavery was done away. Traders and officers are not always so kind as they should be. Any way, the African idea of a white man is *that he is a devil;* and it takes a good deal of intimate association with one who obeys the law of love, and treats him as a brother and an equal, before he begins to feel that a white man *can* be a human brother! Then their cruelty to each other is *the fruit of love*, blinded and maddened by superstition. It is love to each other that makes them seek out and kill those they believe to be witches! Nothing else. I once thought that they *could* not in their hearts *believe* the nonsense of the medicine-men, or that the accused persons were really guilty of death. But I assure you they actually do, and it is equally useless to ridicule them and to blame them. I once said to Lutete, our first convert, a former *nganga*, "Surely you did not really *believe* all that?" "I did indeed," he replied, "*thoroughly*. The devil deceived me as much as that!" If *he* believed it, how much more the common people! Their cruelty is indeed base and cowardly, but it is born of superstition, and superstition is a terrible tyrant.

The Christian of course gives up all that superstition after conversion?

Entirely. His superstitions never once seemed to trouble Lutete after he trusted in Christ. Our house had a ceiling of mats, forming a kind of loft—of which no use was made—under the roof. The natives however believed that in that loft we kept the spirits of all that died of the strange sad "sleeping sickness," which has carried off large numbers in our neighbourhood lately, including twenty of our Church members. It was in vain we tried to show them the folly of the notion, and that there was nothing there. "No, not in the day time, but *at night*—ah!" After Lutete's conversion he came to live near us, because his life was in danger in his own place. But his wife would not come; she was afraid of these spirits, out of which it was alleged we got some profit. Lutete was accused of being a traitor to his people, for the sake of sharing in these fabulous "profits"! After a while he tried to persuade his wife to come and live with him again. "I've been there for weeks, and I've seen no spirits. Come! And I promise you that, if you see them, we will move away." She came, heard the gospel daily, and the Lord soon opened her heart and took away all her fears. We baptized her before long under the name of Lydia. Her husband was called Barnabas, because as my first Christian brother among the natives he was such a comfort to me, a real son of consolation! The people cannot pronounce a terminal *s*, so they call him Barnaba.

Why do you change their names on baptism in that way?

They wish it themselves. They feel they are new creatures, entering on a new life, and they want a new name. Besides many of their names have bad meanings—associated with evil heathen customs. They give us fresh names too, for very often they can't pronounce our English ones. Mine—Richards—is a regular puzzle to them. Both the initial *R* and the final *s* are beyond them. They call me *Uguankasi* or uncle, and my wife *Mundele N'kentu* (white woman), or simply "Mama." Lydia was a thoroughly intelligent woman, and quite understood the difference between flesh and spirit, faith and works, and so on. She was a great help among the women inquirers when my wife was in England.

Do you ever have occasion to excommunicate any of your Church members?

Yes, we have done so four or five times. I do not initiate such action myself. I leave all questions of receiving and rejecting to the Church, because I don't want to make them like children depending on me. I am intensely anxious to develop them as rapidly as possible into a self-governing and self-extending Church. They cannot become this till they have the Scriptures, and can read them. That is why we are pressing on as much as possible with translations. But I teach them to refer everything to Scripture, and decide every case according to its precepts. They perfectly understand that all wicked persons must be put away from among them, and they are inclined to be rather severe. But it is a good fault at first.

What sort of cases do you put away?

One man was put out for marrying a second wife, while his first was alive. The other cases were for immorality. This sin is very common on the Congo, and Christians sometimes fall into it. They will come spontaneously and with tears and shame confess their sin. But the Church is very firm, and puts them away, and keeps them away a long time. They sometimes need to be urged to accept evident contrition and restore the offender. We have had three or four such cases.

How do you manage about polygamy?

If a man is a polygamist when converted we do not make him put away any of his wives. *To do so in Africa would be very wrong.* But we don't allow a Christian to marry more than one of course. They see the benefits of having only one wife, and say, "Ah! it is the devil misleads our people about this." They see that we are far better off with one wife than they are with several. One day an unhappy fellow who had three had somehow offended them all. When he went to the first house —for a husband builds a separate house for each wife—the door was rudely shut in his face. He tried the second, only to be greeted with "Go away, I don't want you!" Nor was the third any more willing to admit him. So he bewailed himself to me and said, "I have three wives, and yet none of them will let me in!" They see our ways, and say: "When you go home, your ife get you cup of tea, make you lie down if tired, nurse you if sick; kind! good! Why does she respect you and be so kind to you? We wish our wives were like that." Then I explain that they must first respect and love their wives and treat them as I do mine. I may say that the Christians do so. One of the first things I observed when Lutete was converted was that he was helping his wife in the field! The people were much struck when they first saw us walking arm in arm. "See!" I overheard them saying, "see! those two are one!"

Are they kind to their children?

The mothers are very much so, and the fathers too, if they are free men, and the children are their own. But so often the father is a slave. Then the children belong to his master, and he does not care much about them. But the mothers are very kind, as a rule. In order to keep the public meetings quieter by dispensing with the babies I once proposed a *crêche*, in which one or two women might mind all the infants. But the idea was laughed to scorn. What! *leave their babies to other people?* Impossible!

Do the Christians take any part in public worship?

Oh, freely! They pray in public—men and women, using at times of course curious expressions. I remember one man when pleading earnestly for holiness said, "Lord, make our hearts pure, make them clean: as clean as a white man's plate!" I could not but smile; but our washing up dishes, and keeping them bright and clean is strange to them, and had struck this man. As to preaching, the converts are some of them really gifted, and speak with great power.

Mr. Ingham wrote to me lately of a boy who has been converted since I left, who can hold in rapt attention an audience of hundreds. Yet Congo folk are like people here: they won't stay in a meeting unless they are interested.

Was that lad one you knew?

Ay! and one I had prayed for, and striven with, and taught, and longed for many a year! A good, bright boy, but an inveterate thief. We could not trust him out of our sight. He seemed to steal for the sake of stealing, even when he could make no use of the thing stolen. Now all is changed. Mr. and Mrs. Ingham are pretty slow to believe in the natives; but they write that this lad is so good, so earnest, and so gifted, that he ought to be sent to America for a good education at one of the Southern colleges. I hope he may be.

Then you believe in educating Congo lads in Europe and America?

No, not as a rule. I think it generally spoils them, and makes them very troublesome. But there are cases of an exceptional character. We must have some high-class native teachers and preachers by-and-by, to be heads of native colleges, and so on. I would prepare a few such lads who can stand it without getting spoiled. Tommy is such a nice bright fellow, that I never could help loving him, even when he was always giving me trouble by his dishonesty. He would be utterly ashamed when convicted or caught, but seemed as if he could not help it. Now grace has altered him; he is honest and trustworthy, and so gifted, that he quite eclipses Lukoke of Lukunga.

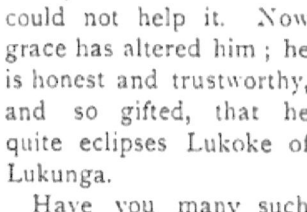

Have you many such preachers?

Not so good; but we

have many. Indeed, all the men feel it their duty to testify for Christ, and some of the women. And they do it to white men as well as black sometimes; for they always ask about any one they meet, "Is he a child of God?" If we cannot say yes, they conclude at once that he is a child of the devil; for they have *no conception of a neutral condition*, and I am not sure but they are right in that! They perfectly distinguish between the two classes, and that the whites differ just as much as they do among themselves. One of our Christians began evangelizing a young officer once. This man wrote and asked me: "What has come over your Banza Manteka men? I can't understand what has changed them so wonderfully. Do tell me." Ah! the grace of God is a wonderful power!

What do you think about flogging as a punishment?

I altogether and unhesitatingly object to it, even for boys. I consider it quite as ungodly to beat an African as an Englishman. What right have we—missionaries, traders, or travellers—to beat men? None whatever. I have seen horrid, blood-curdling cruelties of this kind perpetrated on helpless natives, on women, ay, and on young women too, by traders. But it is wicked, unprincipled, and unjust! We have no more right to commit a personal assault on a naked black man who is willing to work for us, than on a white labourer employed here. It is a remnant of slavery, and a detestable crime. There is no need for it, only selfishness and passion in possession of unbridled power lead to it. Other punishments might be annexed to crime. The natives themselves never thrash anybody. They are very angry if they are struck, and feel it to be a gross insult. I made it a principle never under any provocation to strike man or boy. I believe that Africans should be treated precisely like Europeans; kindly, respectfully, and in a brotherly, manly way. Patronage they hate! We may think ourselves superior, but they do not see it. They often think white men uncommonly poor creatures. We can't do many things they can do, and they don't understand the assumption of Europeans. A white man who strikes a native loses influence with them at once, and can never do them any good. They must be won by love, just like Englishmen. We must forget that they are

JOSEPH CLARKE, OF PALABALA,
AND TWO CHRISTIAN LADS.

black, it makes no real difference. They are men. Even with children, we punish some other way—never by striking.

But what would you do with a naughty boy?

Well, I had trouble with one who had been in England. He was cross and sulky, and wanted toilet soap, if you please, and better food, and I caught him domineering over other boys, and even beating them and making them cry. I took him into my room, reminded him he was only a slave to the king, and of all I had done for him and taught him, upbraided him for ingratitude, and told him decidedly I would have no nonsense. "If I see any more such conduct, I take off your clothes and send you away back to the town to be a slave again." The boy was quite broken down, ashamed, and grieved, and I had no more trouble with him. After the revival I got the king, who set a high price on the lad, to set him free. He is married now, a good Christian man.

Are the children in the schools fairly quick in learning?

Not the little ones. But after five or six years old I should say they are remarkably so. N'snuda, a girl of nine or ten, learned to read well in about eight months; so did Wamba and N'kimba, younger boys, and to do some arithmetic also. One week N'snuda learned by heart perfectly the first, third, and fourth of John. David, a young fellow of twenty, learned to read in public right well. He preached, too, so well that an American lady who heard him said, "If I had known you had such evangelists as that, I do not think I should have come to Africa!"

And you hope to be able to leave the Church at Banza Manteka some day, commending its native elders to God and to the word of His grace?

I do indeed; as soon as they shall have the word of His grace, or the greater part of it. But as yet they have not this by any means. We have the gospels, and parts of Romans and Genesis and other books; but there is very much yet to be done in translation. The language is a most rich and complicated one. Very few missionaries understand it *thoroughly* yet. The people need much instruction before they will be able to stand alone. But really if they had the Bible I should scarcely fear to leave them even now! The Lord would lead them on! They have set apart some of their number as evangelists, and they strongly realize their joyful duty to spread the glad tidings.

That sleeping sickness seems sadly prevalent? Can it not be cured?

No; patients invariably die. The nature of the complaint is not well understood. I think it is a brain disease, from a strange look in the eyes, which I have always noticed as preceding it. The victim becomes stupid after a time, and loses memory and power of motion. Many die too from smallpox. But the State Government has done good by introducing vaccine, and forbidding sick carriers to enter the towns. The people have learned to vaccinate themselves, and villages have been saved from attack by this. But we have lost many members from both diseases. Not unfrequently when a name is mentioned in calling over the roll at a Church meeting the answer comes, "*Balukidi*"—gone up!

APPENDIX A.

List of Present Missionary Agencies in the Congo Free State.

ELEVEN different missionary agencies are already at work in the Congo Free State—three Roman Catholic and eight Protestant.

1. The *Mission du Saint Esprit*, at Banana and Boma, under the care of Mgr. Carrie. Four priests and two lay brethren are connected with this mission, which has small schools, and gives some industrial training to the children.

2. The *Belgian Mission*, established only in 1888 at Kwamouth, on the Upper Congo, and hoping to plant a second station at Luluaberg, on the Kasai, shortly.

3. There is a mission worked by the *Pères d'Algérie* (or Algerian priests) in the south-east part of the Free State. It has two stations at Mpala and Kibango, on Lake Tanganyika, but it does not seem to be having much success. The Romanists are showing more activity in Portuguese territory than in the Free State.

The Protestant missions are :

1. The *Livingstone Inland Mission of the American Baptist Missionary Union*, with seven stations—Mukimvika, opposite Banana on the coast, Palabala, Banza Manteka, and Lukunga, in the Cataract gorge ; and Leopoldville, Bwemba, and Wangata on the upper river. This mission has now about thirty missionaries, and has many schools and chapels, with some hundreds of baptized Church members, including many native preachers. It has a steamer on the upper river, and has prepared, in the various dialects spoken through seven hundred miles of country, many translations from the Scriptures, besides vocabularies, grammars, and school books. It has also medical

missions at Mukimvika and Kinchassa. It has been working for the last twelve years, and exerts a good deal of influence among the natives.

2. The *English Baptist Missionary Society* has seven stations—Tundwa, on the lower river, St. Salvador (Portuguese territory), 'Ngombe, or Lutete, in the Cataract region, and Kinchassa, Bolobo, and Lukolela, on the upper river. The steamer *Peace* belongs to this mission, and in it Mr. Grenfell has done much good service by explorations of many of the tributaries of the Congo. Mr. Bentley, of 'Ngombe, is the author of the best dictionary extant of the Ki-kongo language: and several translations have also been prepared. Mrs. Bentley is endeavouring to teach the natives the working of the telegraph, in preparation for the time when the railway will require young telegraphists. She took back with her from Europe a miniature telegraph line for teaching purposes. Many native converts are connected with this mission, which has also been working twelve years in the country.

3. The excellent *Swedish Missionary Society's* work was originally connected with the Livingstone Inland Mission, and occupied its station of Mukimbungu, between Isanghila and Manyanga; but when the transfer of this Mission to the American Baptist Missionary Union took place in 1884, it was arranged that the Swedes should work an independent mission from that station as a centre, supported and directed from their own country. They have now about twenty missionaries, and have formed two additional stations on the north side of the Congo—Diadia and Kibunzi. They have many converts, Mr. Westlind is a remarkably good linguist, and has translated John's Gospel.

4. *Bishop Taylor's Mission* was formed to work on the great southern tributary of the Congo, the Kasai; but though commenced four years ago (in 1886), with an unusually large first party, consisting of twenty-four missionaries, under the bishop's own leading, it has not yet reached its field of labour, or commenced any missionary work proper. The peculiar plans which were adopted have proved totally unsuited to the country. Very large sums of money were expended on a raft and traction-engine, brought from America, and subsequently on a steamer, so constructed that its heavier portions could not be landed at Vivi or carried up country. None of this machinery has been of any use as yet. The principle of self-support was attempted; and as a result the agents of the mission have suffered great privations, many having died, and others have left the Congo. The rest are scattered around Banana, Vivi, and Isanghila, and are making a brave struggle

to sustain life by shooting hippopotami, and selling the dried flesh to the natives, in exchange for the produce of the country. Four of the party are occupying an old State station at Kimpoko, on Stanley Pool, and attempting a little agriculture and trade ; but none of the would-be missionaries have been able to devote much time to studying the languages, or teaching the people. None of their stations exert as yet any spiritual influence over the neighbouring districts, and consequently no converts have been made. But the mission has not been long at work.

New plans are not always an improvement on old ones ! Nothing can exceed the bishop's cheerful courage and confidence in the ultimate success of his methods, nor his enthusiastic desire to do good in Africa. We hope that he may yet—by somewhat modifying his plans, and adapting them to the backward state of development in the country—succeed in planting his mission on the Kasai. He has come to the conclusion that he will have, like others before him, to found a chain of stations before he can launch a steamer on the Pool, and that the heavy one first taken out is no use for this purpose. He intends to reconstruct and use it on the lower river, where however trading steamers are now plying.

5. A second American agency has tried to follow somewhat on these lines, *The Missionary Evangelical Alliance ;* but its operations, at present, consist only of one small attempt near Vivi, where the missionaries reside in a little native hut, and live by hunting buffalo and antelopes. They smoke the flesh of these animals, and sell it to the natives. It is clear that men who have to support themselves and their families in Africa will never have much time for either study or teaching ! The Congo country is not one for *colonists :* its climate renders it totally unlike South Africa in this respect. For European teachers to live in it *at all* is difficult, and every working hour of their lives ought consequently to be devoted to *direct* missionary work. It is a pity if the Church of Christ, which gives such large sums to sustain its ministers at home, cannot afford to sustain its ministers abroad, and thus liberate them from the necessity of wasting their priceless time and risking their precious lives in order to procure themselves food.

6. In the south-east part of the Congo Free State, among the sources of the Congo in the Garengange country, *Mr. F. S. Arnot* has established his mission. After years of weary peregrinations through the Zambesi and Barotse districts he found this location suitable for the

residence of Europeans. The mission is still in its infancy, though Mr. Arnot has not yet succeeded in making his way back to his station with his wife and new helpers, and in rejoining his colleagues there. It is one of the most interesting and heroic of missions, very far removed from all communication with other Europeans, and hundreds of miles distant from any base of supplies. The climate of Garangange is fairly healthy, and the king of the country friendly. But the immense distance from the coast, and the absence of a connecting chain of stations, make the difficulties, dangers, and expenses very great.

7. The *London Missionary Society's Mission*, on Lake Tanganyika, is also in the Congo Free State. Their stations are KAVALA ISLAND and FWAMBOON, the southern extremity of the lake. This mission, long under the care of Captain Hore (who is now in England), has endured severe trials, and has felt the immense difficulties arising from its remote position—a walk of 800 miles from Zanzibar being involved in getting to the lake. The only other means of access (*viâ* the Zambesi, Shiré, Lake Nyassa, and the Stevenson Road) being, though easier, too precarious to depend upon, and frequently blocked by Arabs. This mission has the steamer *Good News* on the lake, and has done some excellent work in schools and preaching the gospel; but the sphere is a hard one.

8. The *Congo-Balolo Mission*, on the Upper Congo—our own mission born last spring—has selected for its sphere the six southern tributaries of the Congo beyond Equatorville, the Lulonga, Maringa, Lopori, Ikelemba, Juapa, and Bosira, presenting together about 2,000 miles of navigable water-way, with towns and villages on both banks. It has eleven missionaries. The first party reached their destination about six months after leaving England, though taking with them a considerable amount of material for the construction of their first stations. They have the use of the A.B.M.U. steamer *Henry Reed*, kindly lent for a year, before the expiration of which it is hoped their own steamer, the *Pioneer*—sent out in December, 1889, for reconstruction—will be ready for the use of the mission. Mr. and Mrs. McKittrick, Messrs. Whytock, Haupt, Howell, Todd, and Blake, together with Miss de Hailes, formed the first party of this mission. They were reinforced early in 1890 by Messrs. Adamson, Luff, and Cole. The two former went out in charge of the new steamer; and the latter as missionary agriculturist to assist on the Lulonga. The mission has already two stations, Mulonga and Ikau.

When we remember that all this country was unknown eleven years ago, and that the Congo Free State itself dates only from 1885—such an array of agencies, scattered over its vast area already, is a most hopeful sign. Christianity, even in its least pure form, is a vast advance on the cruelties and fetish of Central Africa. In its pure form it is life from the dead.

When the Livingstone Inland Mission began its operations in January, 1878, it stood alone; now it is, thank God! one among a dozen different organizations having the spread of Christianity for their object. We hear also that the American Presbyterians intend to enter the field, which is vast enough—being as large as all India—to welcome a dozen more agencies.

All these missions together only muster about a hundred effective workers, and there are about fifty millions to be evangelized in the Congo Free State alone, and probably five times that number in the rest of unevangelized Africa.

From the last mission station on the Upper Congo, a journey of a thousand miles would be needed to reach the nearest stations on the east—those on the great lakes. Seventeen hundred miles to the northeast lies the Red Sea, and there is no mission station between! Two thousand two hundred miles due north is the Mediterranean, and no mission station between; while two thousand five hundred miles to the north-west are the stations of the North African Mission, but no single centre of light between! Seven hundred miles to the west is the Cameroons Station, but the whole intervening country is unvisited; and in the south-west the American Mission at Bihé is fully a thousand miles distant.

Our Lord Jesus Christ said, "If ye love Me, keep My commandments." His last commandments were:

"GO YE INTO ALL THE WORLD, AND PREACH THE GOSPEL TO EVERY CREATURE." And

"YE SHALL BE WITNESSES UNTO ME . . . UNTO THE UTTERMOST PARTS OF THE EARTH."

HARLEY COLLEGE AND GROUNDS, BOW, LONDON, E.

THE EAST LONDON INSTITUTE
FOR HOME AND FOREIGN MISSIONS.

Founder and Hon. Director:
H. GRATTAN GUINNESS, D.D., F.R.G.S.

Hon. Secretary:
MRS. H. GRATTAN GUINNESS.

Treasurer:
SIR ARTHUR BLACKWOOD.

Bankers:
LONDON AND SOUTH-WESTERN BANK (BOW BRANCH).

Hon. Auditors:
ARTHUR J. HILL, VELLACOTT & Co., Finsbury Circus.

Trustees:
THEODORE HOWARD, ESQ., Westleigh, Bickley, Kent.
CAPT. THE HON. R. MORETON, Hamilton, Ontario.
REV. J. STEPHENS, M.A., Somerset Villa, Dartmouth Park Hill, N.
J. VAN SOMMER, ESQ., 13, New Inn, Strand, W.C.
SIR ARTHUR BLACKWOOD, K.C.B., Shortlands House, Shortlands, Kent.

Hon. London Director:
H. GRATTAN-GUINNESS, M.R.C.S.

THIS Institute was founded in March, 1872, with a view to increase the number of ambassadors for Christ among the heathen, and in the darker regions of Christendom.

THE WORLD'S POPULATION, according to the best estimates, is at present about 1,400 millions. Only about 400 millions are, even in name, Christians, and the remainder of *over a thousand millions* are consequently non-Christians, and for the most part heathen. The greater part of this almost inconceivable mass have never heard of Christ, and have little chance of doing so, for Protestant missionaries are scattered among them only in the proportion of ONE to every three or four hundred thousand. No single individual could possibly minister the word of life to such a multitude, even in Christendom ; how much less in heathendom !

THE SUPPLY IS CLEARLY INADEQUATE, and yet the evangelical Churches at home are rich both in men and money. There is no reason why it should not speedily be doubled, trebled, multiplied tenfold. There are in our home Churches thousands of converted and devoted young men and women suitable for missionaries, and willing to become such ; and there is wealth enough in the hands of Christians to send them forth and sustain them among the heathen. Some of these are educated, and have already engaged more or less in the service of God in this land, and having means of their own, can go forth into heathendom when they will. Others hear the call of God, and desire to obey, but lack the needful education, and have neither leisure nor means to acquire it, nor the ability to go forth at their own charges.

OUR INSTITUTE seeks to arouse men and women of this latter class, to hear and heed the last great command of Christ : it helps them to fit themselves for service in heathendom, or in other needy spheres, by offering them, freely, a course of suitable study and practical training. It then introduces them to the field for which they seem best adapted, and, if need be, sustains or helps to sustain them in it. It seeks also, and in order to all this, the diffusion of information by press and platform as to the world's wants and the Lord's work, so as to deepen in the hearts of Christians at home *practical compassion for the heathen* and a sense of *responsibility to give them the gospel.*

TWO COLLEGES, each adapted for fifty men—one in East London and the other in North Derbyshire—

are connected with the Institute, which has also a TRAINING HOME FOR THIRTY YOUNG WOMEN STUDENTS preparing for missionary work. The course of study and practical training is adapted to afford the students such help as they are capable of receiving, and as will fit them for future usefulness in the sphere to which they may seem best adapted. It extends over three years, and, in the case of regular medical students, over a longer time. *All* the students receive a certain measure of medical preparation, both theoretical and practical.

AN EXTENSIVE HOME MISSION WORK, in which the students receive practical training, is carried on in connexion with the Institute, among the working classes in East London. Its operations comprise a medical mission with a numerously attended dispensary, and a maternity department worked under a certificated lady by the young women students; mothers' meetings; night schools for men, for lads, and for factory girls; a soup kitchen; Band of Hope and temperance meetings; house-to-house visitation, open-air preaching, tent meetings in summer, Sunday schools and Bible classes, and gospel preaching. Two mission halls in Bow and Bromley, with schoolrooms and classrooms attached, are worked directly and exclusively by the Institute, and the students help in a large number of other mission halls, and preach also in churches and chapels.

THE INSTITUTE IS BROADLY CATHOLIC IN ITS PRINCIPLES AND PRACTICE; it trains men of all evangelical *denominations*, of all *nationalities*, and of all *classes;* and it trains them for all societies, all lands, and all spheres of Christian effort. It is as comprehensive as it is possible to be, within the limits of evangelical truth. It seeks to be GODLY and practical in character and in methods: to cultivate devotion, dependence on God, self-denial, self-support as far as possible, and self-sacrifice ; and it aims especially at " the regions beyond," or neglected and unevangelized fields at home and abroad.

THE STUDENTS HAVE BEEN OF VARIOUS NATIONALITIES : not only English, Scotch, Irish, and American, but French, German, Italian, Spanish, Swedish, Danish, Russian, Bulgarian, Syrian, Egyptian, Kaffir, Negro, Hindu, Parsi, Kurdish, and Jewish. They have also been of various denominations. The large majority of those who have gone out as missionaries are now connected with about twenty different societies and associations, while a number are working ndependently as self-sustaining missionaries, medical or otherwise.

MORE THAN FIVE HUNDRED MISSIONARIES, former students in the Institute, are now labouring in China, India, Syria, Armenia, Egypt ; in France, Spain, Portugal, Italy ; East, West, North, South, and Central Africa, in Natal and Cape Colony ; in Prince Edward's Isle, Cape Breton, Canada, and the Western States of America ; in the West Indies, Brazil, and the Argentine Republic ; in Australia and New Zealand ; as well as in various parts of the home mission field. The object of the Institute is especially to send evangelists to " the regions beyond " those already evangelized.

ONE HUNDRED AND TWENTY STUDENTS are now in training, and some of their number are continually passing out into the great world-field. One every week, on an average, enters on active missionary life.

Contributions in aid of any of the objects of the Institute may be sent either to the Treasurer, SIR ARTHUR BLACKWOOD, K.C.B., Shortlands House, Shortlands, Kent ; or to the Secretary, MRS. H. GRATTAN GUINNESS, Harley House, Bow, London, E., from whom fuller information can be had on application.

The Congo-Balolo Mission

is formed for the evangelization of the millions of Balolo people dwelling in the great horseshoe-shaped territory of the Upper Congo, and accessible by its southern affluents, the Lulonga, Lopori, Maringa, Ikelemba, Juapa, and Bosira.

It is a continuation and extension of the Livingstone Inland Mission, commenced in 1878, and now occupying and working a chain of seven Stations from the Coast to the Equator.

It was founded in the spring of 1889, and has eleven Missionaries, two Stations, and the steamer *Pioneer*.

DIRECTORATE.
THE MANAGERS OF THE EAST LONDON INSTITUTE.

TREASURER.
Sir ARTHUR BLACKWOOD, K.C.B., Shortlands House, Kent.

BANKERS.
THE LONDON AND COUNTY BANKING COMPANY, LIMITED, Lombard Street, E.C.

HON. AUDITORS.
ARTHUR J. HILL, VELLACOTT & CO., Finsbury Circus.

HON. SECRETARY.
H. GRATTAN GUINNESS, Jun., M.R.C.S., Harley House, Bow, E.

ADVISORY COUNCIL.
Rev. ARCHIBALD G. BROWN, 22, Bow Road, E.
P. S. BADENOCH, Esq., Mildmay Conference Hall, N.
RICHARD CORY, Esq., Oscar House, Cardiff.
Dr. H. GRATTAN and Mrs. GUINNESS, Cliff House, Curbar, *via* Sheffield.
Mr. and Mrs. H. GRATTAN GUINNESS, Jun., Harley House, Bow, E.
Miss L. GUINNESS, Cliff House, Curbar, *via* Sheffield.
RICHARD HILL, Esq., 3, Lombard Court, E.C.
E. J. KENNEDY, Esq., Exeter Hall, W.C.
Dr. MACRAE, 1, Bow Road, E.
W. SEAGRAM, Esq., 86, Piccadilly, W.

Just Published. Second and enlarged Edition of

Coloured Map, Portrait, and numerous Illustrations. In cloth, price 5s. Direct from Harley House, post free, 3s. 6d. In boards, 4s.; post free, 2s. 6d.

"Instinct with life. Yet all is told so gently and with such effusiveness of love for the work, that many, we hope, may be led to recognise the beauty of individual self-devotion, animated by a principle so lofty as to be able to sustain itself undaunted, in view of difficulties that, to human sight, might well be deemed invincible. The volume is beautifully illustrated."—*Scottish Guardian.*

"A beautifully prepared and tastefully illustrated book on Chinese mission work. The evident sincerity breathed in every line, and the spiritual needs of the vast Chinese empire lying as a heavy burden on the writer's heart, find constant expression in burning words of self-consecration and appeal."—*Methodist Recorder.*

"Very bright and graphic letters, . . . charmingly 'got up,' under skilful editorship; . . . altogether most attractive. The very thing to read aloud."—*Church Missionary Intelligencer.*

"A choice and dainty volume, beautifully illustrated with pictures of Chinese life and scenery. The letters are worthy of the setting, being natural and picturesque descriptions of missionary travel, life, and work, bringing China and its millions home to us in all their need. The tone is high and earnest."—*Church of Scotland Mission Record.*

"I have been dipping into your *so beautiful* 'In the Far East,' with my dim, dim eyes."—*Dr. Davia Brown.*

"Thank you most sincerely for sending me this book. I have read it with great interest, and will do what little is in my power to make its burning pages known."—*Professor Henry Drummond.*

"The best account of the first experiences of China to a traveller and missionary that I have ever met with; altogether beside their value for deep piety. The extreme taste and beauty of the illustrations and general get up of the volume leave nothing to be desired."—*Rev. F. B. Meyer, M.A.*

"I have greatly enjoyed 'In the Far East.' God blessing it, the book should send armies of believers to invade the Flowery Land. Your sister is happy in her editor. God bless you, and all the beloved household. Yours heartily."—*C. H. Spurgeon.*

"The gift of writing well for the great cause of missions, joined with the consecrated art of working well therefor, we see admirably exhibited in this little volume. The earlier letters of the collection we were privileged to hear read in the English home from which the beloved daughter went forth, and to which she sent back these glowing records of her evangelistic journeyings and labours. We were deeply impressed then, as we have been in the re-reading, with the graphic beauty and evangelical richness of these missionary epistles. They are worthy of publication for the spirit which is in them, for the information which they convey, and for the fire which they are sure to communicate to Christian hearts by the burning zeal which kindles in their every word and sentence."—*A. J. Gordon.*

The following works, in various Congo languages, have been prepared, among others, by members of the mission:

A SMALL DICTIONARY OF THE LANGUAGE (English-Congo and Congo-English); together with a list of useful sentences for Missionaries and Travellers in the Congo Cataract Region. By the late HENRY CRAVEN and JOHN BARFIELD, B.A. 248 pages.

THE FIRST EPISTLE OF JOHN, EXODUS XX., AND GENESIS I.-III. Translated into Ki-kongo. By T. H. HOSTE.

A VOCABULARY OF KILOLO, as spoken by the Bankundu, a section of the Balolo tribe, at Ikengo (Equator), Upper Congo. With a few Introductory Notes on the Grammar. By J. B. EDDIE. 200 pages.

A GRAMMAR OF THE CONGO LANGUAGE, as spoken 200 years ago. Translated from the Latin of Brusciotto. Edited by H. GRATTAN GUINNESS, D.D. 112 pages.

A GRAMMAR OF THE CONGO LANGUAGE, as now spoken in the Cataract Region below Stanley Pool. By H. GRATTAN GUINNESS, D.D. 267 pages, 8vo.

MOSAIC HISTORY AND GOSPEL STORY, Epitomised in the Congo Language. By H. GRATTAN GUINNESS, D.D. 87 pages, 8vo.

THE CONCORDS OF THE CONGO LANGUAGE. Being a Contribution to the Syntax of the Congo Tongue. By JOHN BARFIELD, B.A. 160 pages, small 8vo.

THE PEEP OF DAY, translated into the Ki-kongo Language. By J. B. EDDIE.

THE PEEP OF DAY, translated into N'Kundu, a dialect of the Kilolo Language, as spoken at the Equator, Upper Congo. By J. B. EDDIE. 120 pages.

THE GOSPEL OF ST. MARK, translated into the Ki-kongo Language. By C. H. HARVEY. 98 pages.

KIBANGI VOCABULARY. By A. SIMS, M.B. 111 pages.

YALULEMA VOCABULARY. By A. SIMS, M.B. 35 pages.

CONGO READING BOOK. 96 pages.

THE GOSPEL OF ST. LUKE, translated into the Ki-kongo Language. By H. RICHARDS. 154 pages.

ST. MATTHEW V.-VII. (*Mataiona*), translated into Ki-kongo.

EXODUS (*Wavaikulu*), translated into Ki-kongo. By CHAS. E. INGHAM. 89 pages.

Two Reading Books, compiled by C. E. INGHAM, consist of the following:

No. 1. **HOME LESSONS**, by Mrs. INGHAM. Short Sentences, etc. Collection of Congo Fables.

No. 2. **HOME LESSONS.** Genesis i.-iii.; Romans i., ii.; Luke i., ii.; Sermon on Mount; Romans viii.; Hymns.

1. **GENESIS I.-XXII.** By C. E. INGHAM.
2. **MATTHEW I.-XI.** By H. RICHARDS.
3. **JOHN'S GOSPEL.** By WESTLIND, S.M.S.
4. **MARK'S GOSPEL.** By CAMERON, of B.M.S.
5. **THE ACTS OF THE APOSTLES.** By NKOIYO, A.B.M.U.
6. **KITEKE VOCABULARY.** By A. SIMS, M.B. As spoken by the Beteke and kindred tribes of the Upper Congo. 190 pages.
7. **THE EPISTLE TO THE ROMANS.** By H. GRATTAN GUINNESS, D.D. assisted by NKOIYO.
8. **THE FIRST EPISTLE OF JOHN.** By H. GRATTAN GUINNESS, D.D., assisted by NKOIYO.
9. **JOHN'S GOSPEL.** By A. SIMS, M.B. Translated into Kiteke.

Regions Beyond.

MONTHLY ORGAN OF THE

East London Institute for Home and Foreign Missions,

AND OF THE

Balolo Mission to the Upper Congo.

EDITED BY

MRS. H. GRATTAN GUINNESS.

CONTAINS

LEADING ARTICLES on Missionary Questions.
NOTICES of Unevangelized Nations and Newly Opened Spheres.
Current MISSIONARY NEWS, and Special Notice of all ADVANCE in AFRICA.
TIDINGS from former Students of the East London Institute, now working in various parts of the World.
The Record of the CONGO-BALOLO MISSION.
Letters from MISS GUINNESS in China.
Accounts of HOME MISSION WORK, especially that of the East London Institute.
POETRY, MUSIC, PORTRAITS, MAPS, and ILLUSTRATIONS.

London:
S. W. PARTRIDGE & CO., 9, PATERNOSTER ROW, E.C.

America:
TREMONT TEMPLE, BOSTON, MASS.

Works by Dr. & Mrs. H. GRATTAN GUINNESS.

THE DIVINE PROGRAMME OF THE WORLD'S HISTORY. By Dr. and Mrs. H. GRATTAN GUINNESS. Demy 8vo, cloth, 7s. 6d. Direct from the Authors, post free, for 6s. 2d.

LIGHT FOR THE LAST DAYS: a Study, Historical and Prophetical. By Dr. and Mrs. H. GRATTAN GUINNESS. In 8vo, cloth, with two Coloured Diagrams, price 7s. 6d. Direct from the Authors, post free for 6s. 2d.

ROMANISM AND THE REFORMATION. From the Standpoint of Prophecy. By Dr. H. GRATTAN GUINNESS. In cloth, crown 8vo, price 5s. Direct from the Author, post free, for 4s. 2d.

THE APPROACHING END OF THE AGE. Viewed in the Light of History, Prophecy, and Science. By Dr. H. GRATTAN GUINNESS, F.R.G.S. Tenth edition, in one large volume, with four Diagrams, crown 8vo, 700 pages, cloth, price 7s. 6d. Direct from the Author, post free, for 6s. 2d.

FALLACIES OF FUTURISM. By Dr. and Mrs. H. GRATTAN GUINNESS. 93 pages, demy 8vo. For distribution, 3d. each. Single copies, post free, price 6d.

THE WEEK AND ITS ORIGIN. By Dr. H. GRATTAN GUINNESS, F.R.G.S. A Reply to the Article of the Bishop of Carlisle in the *Contemporary Review*. Price, post free, 3d.

THE HERESY OF THE REV. G. O. BARNES (the "Kentucky Evangelist") Exposed and Answered. By H. GRATTAN GUINNESS. Price, post free, 2d.

SHE SPAKE OF HIM. Being Recollections of the loving Labours and Early Death of Mrs. Henry Dening. By Mrs. GUINNESS. Seventh Edition, with nine Illustrations. 256 pages, large 8vo. Price, in cloth, post free, 1s. 6d.

LEAFLET PACKET (*New Edition*). Containing Twenty-four Assorted and Illustrated MISSIONARY LEAFLETS. By Mrs. H. GRATTAN GUINNESS. Suitable for inclosing in letters. Price, post free, 6d.

THE NEW WORLD OF CENTRAL AFRICA: Its Condition and Claims on Christians. Including a History of the LIVINGSTONE INLAND MISSION. With Maps, Portraits, and Illustrations. By Mrs. GRATTAN GUINNESS. Price, post free, 5s.

www.ingramcontent.com/pod-product-compliance
Lightning Source LLC
Chambersburg PA
CBHW020135170426
43199CB00010B/758